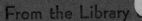

Performance Objectives for School Principals:

Concepts and Instruments

Edited by

Jack A. Culbertson
Curtis Henson
and
Ruel Morrison

McCutchan Publishing Corporation
2526 Grove Street
Berkeley, California 94704

ISBN: 0-8211-0223-0
Library of Congress Catalog Card Number: 74-75367

PREFACE

This book is influenced by and is designed to contribute to four significant trends now affecting the school principalship. These trends include the increasing significance of the school principal's role in education, the developing interest in the continuing education and preservice preparation of principals, the growing focus upon performance objectives for principals, and the enhanced search through school system-university partnerships to define and relate effective performance measures to preparation.

The growing significance of the principalship role in education is being facilitated in various school systems through processes of decentralization designed to give principals greater leadership responsibility. In addition, citizens are looking to principals increasingly to demonstrate leadership within a context of changing school-community relationships. Performance objectives are set forth in this book to highlight special opportunities which principals have to exercise school and community leadership. These objectives are described in all of the domains of behavior treated in this volume, especially in the chapters entitled "Initiating and Responding to Change," and "Preparing the Organization for Effective Response."

Since expectations for enhanced principal leadership are growing, it is understandable that greater attention is being directed toward improving the performance of principals through continuing education. One result is a growing array of approaches for dealing with the continuing education problem. The approach to continuing education elaborated in this book rests upon the following basic assumption: namely, that data-gathering instruments related to performance objectives can be developed and used to acquire information for diagnosing the continuing education needs of principals; further, such diagnoses suggest needed educational experiences for principals. We also believe the concepts and instruments presented provide means to improve diagnostic procedures, which would, in turn, make continuing education for school principals more effective.

The growing focus upon administrative performance and upon more systematic efforts to make explicit performance objectives and criteria reflects a need to achieve more rational decisions and actions in administrative practice and administrator preparation. More specifically, the trend denotes a search for clearer ideas about the purposes and objectives of preparatory programs, including their relationship to administrative practice, and about means which logically relate to these purposes and objectives. Although some would question this approach, it seems unlikely that professional schools and school systems, which ultimately must be concerned with wise and effective action, can turn their back on efforts to clarify the purposes of preparation and practice and to improve the performances needed to achieve these purposes. We believe that the concepts and instruments presented in this publication, which are performance-based in their orientation, demonstrate the logical validity of the general approach.

This book also reflects the trend toward greater use of school system-university partnerships to confront leadership problems facing principals and other school leaders, a trend related to the growth of knowledge bearing upon leadership practices as well as to the increased visibility, if not difficulty, of problems of practice. It is significant that the initiation and design of efforts leading to this publication had their origins in principalship practice within the Atlanta school system. The talent brought to bear upon the effort involved leaders both in school systems and in universities. We believe that the model of university-school system cooperation and the involvement of talent achieved in the University Council for Educational Administration (UCEA)-Atlanta school system effort is unique, and it has implications for future cooperative endeavors. We also believe the concepts and instruments produced can be used to assess and improve principal performance in general.

In sum, then, the book is directed toward the principalship. It should prove useful to those concerned with the continuing education of practicing principals as well as to those in institutions of higher education engaged in the preservice education of principals. It can serve both as a text for higher education courses and as a guide to learning experiences for practicing principals. Chapter One, for example, suggests uses of ideas and instruments by those in school systems desiring to improve the continuing education of principals and offers suggestions for interested leaders in institutions of higher education who desire to update or redesign preparatory programs for principals.

Clearly, the need to improve preservice, resident preparatory programs, as well as in-service programs for principals in school systems, continues to be marked. We hope the concepts and instruments presented here will not only stimulate and help those interested in meeting such needs but that they will also point the way to needed new research and development.

ACKNOWLEDGMENTS

We acknowledge with appreciation the federal funds which were made available to the Atlanta Public School System and which proved to be of marked help in implementing the UCEA-Atlanta Project and preparing the publication which resulted. Specific recognition is accorded the Emergency School Assistance Program (OEG-4-71-0668) for support received.

We are especially indebted to the authors who contributed to this volume. Their special achievements in addressing the challenge they accepted speak fully for their efforts. Recognition is also due members of the "Reaction Panel." They not only provided ideas which influenced this publication; they also helped in several meetings to define and implement the project from which the publication came.

Members of the panel were: George Brain, Washington State University; Benjamin Dowd, George Peabody College; Sidney Estes, Atlanta University; John Greer, Georgia State University; Daniel E. Griffiths, New York University; Andrew E. Hayes, University of North Carolina; Theodore Jones, Atlanta School System; John Martin, Auburn University; Michael Martin, University of Colorado; Rodney W. Pirtle, Highland Park Independent School District (Texas); William Russell, Atlanta School System; Wilson Smith, Saginaw

School District (Michigan); Dolphus Spence, Nashville Metropolitan Public Schools; Lonnie Wagstaff, Ohio State University; James R. Yates, UCEA.

We would also like to express appreciation to the dozens of principals, central office staff, and teachers in Atlanta, who helped in field testing a number of the instruments included in this volume. Although we are not able to recognize all these individuals specifically, we are indebted to them.

Finally, we offer our thanks to Harriet Ferrell, who not only provided important clerical help in the production of this volume but also contributed in other ways to the UCEA-Atlanta Project.

CONTRIBUTORS

Max G. Abbott, Director, Center for Educational Policy and Management, University of Oregon

Dale L. Bolton, Professor of Educational Administration, University of Washington

Jack Culbertson, Executive Director, University Council for Educational Administration

Alan K. Gaynor, Professor of Educational Administration, Boston University

E. Curtis Henson, Assistant Superintendent, Career Education, Atlanta Public Schools

Larry W. Hughes, Professor of Educational Administration, University of Tennessee

James M. Lipham, Professor of Educational Administration, University of Wisconsin

Kenneth E. McIntyre, Professor of Educational Administration, University of Texas

R. Ruel Morrison, Superintendent, Area III, Atlanta Public Schools

James F. Small, Assistant Director, Boston University Human Relations Laboratory (New York Branch)

CONTENTS

Figures

ONE

UCEA AND THE ATLANTA SYSTEM: A CONFLUENCE OF INTERESTS

Jack Culbertson, Curtis Henson, and *Ruel Morrison*

The UCEA-Atlanta Project had its origins in two independent interests that fused. One began within the University Council for Educational Administration (UCEA). The other developed within the Atlanta public school system. The UCEA interest was prompted by an awareness of problems facing urban school leaders. The Atlanta public school system was concerned with designing effective staff development experiences for principals. The studies that appear in this volume are a result of the joining of the two interests.

THE UCEA INTEREST

A major objective which UCEA began to pursue as soon as it came into being in the late 1950's was a broadened base of preparation for educational administrators. This objective, which received major attention throughout the 1960's, focused upon increased use in preparatory programs of content from such social science disciplines as political science, economics, sociology, social psychology, and anthropology.[1] It also encouraged the use of management and planning concepts developed by scholars concerned with business, hospital, government, and educational administration.

Social science content served different purposes in preparatory programs. Some institutions used it to sensitize prospective administrators to important dimensions of the setting within which they were to work. These institutions, in an effort to help administrators understand communities, incorporated content from sociology on social-class structure or content from political science on community conflict, for example. Other institutions tried to help school administrators understand decision making with regard to specific problems; they selected and applied pertinent concepts to case problems and to simulated decision situations. Still other institutions provided a solid grounding in one social science discipline in the hope that a prospective administrator would achieve the perspective needed to address a wide range of decision problems systematically.

During the 1960's a substantial number of management and planning concepts were developed and disseminated by graduate schools concerned with business, government, and educational administration. Although these concepts were often shaped by ideas and methods from the social sciences, they were consistently and directly oriented toward administrative decision-making situations, which is not always true of concepts originating within social science disciplines.

Different studies have shown that many institutions of higher education made substantial progress in incorporating social science and management concepts into their preparatory programs during this decade.[2] Content from sociology was used most frequently by UCEA universities, and content from political science came next. Concepts on management planning were also incorporated into many UCEA university programs.[3]

During the latter half of the decade, especially, an array of forces began to affect universities and school systems[4] and to create a need for adaptation both in school systems and in universities. Pressure for change and improvement, undoubtedly felt most urgently by urban school leaders, increased the need for guiding concepts and experimental techniques beyond those in their immediate environment. Need for change was also felt in institutions of higher education. In the late 1960's, UCEA, with the help of professors and administrators, began to search for new ways to use social science and management concepts by taking those previously used in programs for preparing educational administrators and applying them to administrative problems. Thus, "Project Application," which evolved under

UCEA auspices, was designed to create new approaches to applying such knowledge within school systems. It led to contacts and discussions with leaders in the Atlanta public school system, and out of these discussions emerged a confluence of interests.

THE ATLANTA INTEREST

With the advent of the Elementary and Secondary Education Act (ESEA) in 1965, the Atlanta school system, along with many others in the United States, had additional funds to be spent specifically for enriching and improving basic instructional programs. Utopia had arrived! All the things that schoolmen had said could be done and would be done to bring about miraculous changes in the quality of the instructional program were now possible. Or were they? With the extra funds made available, gadgets, printed materials, audiovisual materials, and other supplies were purchased; consultants were hired; scholarships were provided; in-service education was administered; additional personnel to supervise and assist were employed. But the problem of inadequate education was still with us.

As soon as one problem was solved, another more serious one arose to take its place. The range of abilities, characteristics, and needs of the pupils seemed to be broadening, and traditional instructional programs required more than another educational Band-Aid. Major overhaul or drastic surgery was indicated, and attempts were made to design curriculum programs that would individualize instruction for students. Because colleges continued to prepare teachers in large groups where the lecture method was used, however, in-service courses and preservice training generally failed to demonstrate individualized instruction.

While the paradox of teacher training opportunities and the necessity for individualizing instruction was only one of many recurring problems, it was viewed as the one that had major implications for the entire educational process. In the Atlanta school system, there was a general assumption that teachers teach as they have been taught.

The rationale and a framework for a competency-based teacher education program had been projected at the University of Georgia, but details and specifics had not been worked out. Atlanta teachers joined forces with the university to develop teacher education proficiency modules in the areas of reading and mathematics. Workshops utilizing these modules were designed so that individual teacher needs were diagnosed and assignments were prescribed in a manner identical to that which the teacher was expected to follow in the classroom. To evaluate successfully the results of this program, assessment instruments of teacher performance were needed. Teacher performance criteria, which spelled out in observable, measurable terms what "good" teachers should be doing in their classrooms, were developed. When applied to teachers, these criteria provided the basis for determining their in-service needs.

The success of this program did not stop with Atlanta teachers, however. Other areas of school operation were considered in terms of the value of a competency-based improvement program, and a number of innovative projects conducted by the Atlanta system pointed to the critical role of the principal in program organization and implementation. Experience further demonstrated that the principal was the single most important factor in setting school climate and attaining school goals. If the characteristics of a "good" teacher could be stated in performance terms, could the same be done for principals? Are there certain traits which "good" administrators have in common which mark them as successful? Are there certain observable processes that the "good" principal follows in establishing priorities, in developing faculty communication networks, and in making decisions that differentiate him from his colleagues? If such traits or processes exist, can they be isolated and listed in performance criteria terms or competencies that are measurable and teachable?

Atlanta's progress in answering questions from the teacher's point of view certainly did not provide answers to the questions as applied to the principal. The success achieved with teachers did, however, suggest that such questions could be addressed, that behaviors could be isolated, and that criteria could be established. Furthermore, the possibilities suggested by the competency approach to the principal's role provided unlimited opportunities to improve educational opportunities through improving the principal's function. Atlanta personnel concluded that the criteria, when developed, would be especially helpful to principals in two ways. First, the principal, by using the criteria, would have a valuable tool for self-evaluation and for direction. This use seemed significant because of the established view that self-evaluation is one effective means of improvement. Such criteria could help the principal identify his or her priorities, isolate areas of special need, and enable him or her to request necessary assistance and guidance. The results achieved in such a program might be quite different from those accruing from merely taking another course in educational administration. Second, such criteria could serve as a screening tool in the selection of principals. As a screening tool, it would provide realistic and concrete criteria for assessing administrative talent.

While those in the Atlanta system hoped that the task could be done, it was obviously a formidable one. The myriad of variables involved in administration would require a pool of scholars and practitioners possessing expertise in many areas. The challenge was too great for a single university, a group of universities, a single school system, or a group of school systems. A national network of talent was required. To provide such a resource, the Atlanta public school system turned to UCEA to provide that network. The interest grew out of need as well as success; the response to the challenge grew out of the cooperation that ensued.

DEVELOPMENT OF LONG-RANGE OBJECTIVES

UCEA and Atlanta leaders very early discussed objectives of interest and significance to both agencies. Four long-range development objectives were identified. Two of these objectives were more directly related to the interests of leaders within UCEA. Leaders in both organizations agreed, however, that all objectives were important and that they should be mutually pursued by Atlanta and UCEA personnel. They also recognized that it would take years to achieve the objectives fully.

The first objective, as already implied, was to inaugurate a new system of continuing education for Atlanta's school principals. Not only did leaders in the Atlanta school system agree that school principals were key individuals in any efforts to achieve educational improvement, but they also offered evidence that the principals were increasingly interested in having better opportunities to acquire skills and ideas related to the challenges they were facing and the objectives they were pursuing. In projecting the kind of continuing education system for principals that would be most desirable, several criteria were established: Continuing education should be based upon information related to principal performance and to the settings in which they find themselves. Continuing education, in other words, should be problem-oriented and focused upon skills and understandings needed in practice. Also, continuing education activities should be designed to help principals achieve the objectives they are pursuing more effectively. And, finally, any staff development system should recognize both the strengths and the needs of principals in the design of learning experiences. More specifically, it might prove desirable to create situations within which the identified strengths of principals could be optimally expressed and further developed; in other cases, learning experiences might be directed toward meeting limitations principals have as they face the challenge of effectively attaining objectives.

A second objective, indirectly related to the first, was to develop a more effective system for identifying prospective principals to fill vacated or newly created posts in Atlanta. Again, several criteria were established related to this objective: Any program for assessing administrative potential should be related to the objectives that principals are expected to perform. Any program for assessing potential data should also take into consideration the extent to which prospective candidates can demonstrate a capacity for achieving objectives. The final criterion was that any talent assessment program, to be useful, should develop and state measures of performance related to the objectives of desired principal behavior.

The third objective established for the project was that of developing ideas of use to those in universities concerned with the redesign of preservice programs for principals. Recently there has been an increasing interest on the part of university personnel in the development of performance-based programs for principals that reflect more clearly the challenges of changing practice. Thus, the UCEA-Atlanta Project, because of its focus upon the objectives of principal behavior and criteria related to behavior, was judged to relate directly to the aspirations of a growing number of professors in institutions of higher education. Put differently, the attainment of more clearly defined objectives of principal behavior and the development of instruments related to these objectives would have direct implications for designing resident preparatory programs. Statements delineating objectives of principal behavior, for example, could serve as an important stepping-stone to statements of instructional objectives in preparatory programs. Instructional objectives, in turn, could serve as guides for defining understandings and skills needed to achieve objectives and, in turn, for creating or retrieving the kinds of instructional materials necessary to foster defined skills and understandings. Thus, there seemed to be a clear relationship between developing a system of continuing education for practicing principals and attaining newly designed preservice programs for prospective principals.

The fourth objective was that of discovering more effective approaches to applying knowledge to problems facing educational leaders. This objective was central to UCEA's originally stated interest. The organization hoped to create boundary-spanning arrangements that would link university and school district personnel in mutually beneficial and effective ways in a significant development effort. On the one hand, the Atlanta school system provided an unusual laboratory in which to involve individuals with special talents in applying knowledge and solving problems. On the other hand, UCEA offered a wide range of talent from which to draw. Here was a special opportunity to design and assess that involved an urban school system and talented individuals from a wide range of universities. The individuals involved would share in a challenging developmental experience and evolve approaches to knowledge application that would have implications for interested school systems beyond Atlanta.

ACTION GUIDELINES

Given the four long-range objectives just stated, what strategy might best be used to pursue them? Several things had to be considered before this question could be answered or pertinent actions could be taken. Some of these are discussed in relation to the guidelines stated below. These guidelines were designed to shape actions to be taken in the Atlanta context. They were also stated in terms judged applicable for creating and testing boundary-spanning arrangements involving institutions of higher education and other school systems.

Given the commitment to address significant problems facing educational leaders and given the complexity of knowledge application processes, team rather than individual efforts offered the most promising approach to a strategy. It was agreed that the developmental efforts projected would require the addressing of significant rather

than trivial problems and that the problems likely to be encountered
in the pursuit of the long-range objectives described above would be
very complex.

Given this orientation, it was clear that a range of skills would be
required and that, if the efforts were to prove effective, a "critical
mass" of talent would need to be assembled. Individuals working
with independent orientations would not be able to achieve effective
development. Rather, a team of developers made up of carefully selected individuals with the unique skills required to confront the
complex tasks to be performed would be necessary. A conception
that would integrate dimensions of the tasks to be performed in
some larger developmental pattern was also needed. Put differently, a
pattern involving a succession of unrelated individual efforts would
be unlikely to contribute to the attainment of long-range goals.

*Temporary rather than permanent structures for organizing team
efforts provided the soundest basis for development.* Universities can
be viewed as relatively permanent structures, as can colleges or de-
partments within these institutions. They exist to perform continuing and well-established functions. The same thing can be said for
public school systems and subsystems within them. It seemed desirable to evolve a different structure for the development team, one
that was more temporary than permanent. This meant bringing together a team of selected individuals from different permanent structures of school systems and universities to achieve specified purposes
within defined time periods and then dissolving the team. Team
members would be problem-centered in their work rather than func-
tion-centered. Their authority would be derived much more from the
competence they brought to the task than from the position they
held in the organization within which they resided.[5] It was also assumed that the learning achieved by individuals would be taken back
and applied within their more permanent environments after they
had completed specified tasks within temporary systems.

*Special brokerage arrangements for recruiting and bringing togeth-
er talented individuals in development teams were needed in order to
create temporary systems.* An agency for evolving brokerage arrangements that could span both universities and school systems was
needed. Various agencies might have performed this function, but
UCEA had some immediate advantages. First, within the universities
comprising UCEA were approximately a thousand professors of edu-

cational administration, making available countless combinations of knowledge, experience, and skill that would not be available, for example, to a single university interested in creating brokerage arrangements. Such a pool not only provided opportunities for myriad combinations of talents; it also offered a large reserve for continuing efforts at applied development related to the objectives already noted. A second advantage stemmed from UCEA's past experience in working with development teams through temporary systems.

Any strategy of application, it was agreed, should be continually addressed to a succession of outcomes that could likely be realized. Great expectations for "radical" or "far-reaching" changes in schools have been created in the last decade. Government programs, for example, have roused hopes for major solutions to urban problems of poverty, race, and education. It has become increasingly clear, however, that answers to problems in the urban educational environment are not easy to achieve and that even the most effective approaches to intervention and development cannot be expected to achieve miraculous results immediately. Thus, the approach chosen for defining expectations was clearly important. Both "Band-Aid" and "utopian" approaches had to be eschewed. Serious efforts to create a dynamic that would be meaningful to principals, and, more important, that would reach and affect the fiber of organizational life in schools were needed.

The problem of realistic aspirations was also recognized and assessed. On the one hand, there was considerable risk in achieving a succession of activities that would lead to the full realization of the longer-range objectives. On the other hand, any tendency to state immediate outcome in terms that would clearly force development teams into incompetence or failure should be avoided. Careful attention had to be given to the staging and sequencing of efforts so that realistic and incremental steps toward the longer-range objectives could be taken.

MEANS FOR ACHIEVING MORE IMMEDIATE OUTCOMES

What outcomes bearing upon the long-range objectives should be addressed immediately? The performance of two tasks was basic to the entire effort: one was articulating the desired objectives of principal behavior; the other was evolving concepts necessary for identifying principal performance indicators related to objectives. The means had to relate to these two basic tasks.

Two somewhat different approaches to the tasks of defining desired objectives for principals and criteria of performance were available. One approach, more inductive in nature, would have focused upon the gathering of data about principal behavior in Atlanta and the policy objectives of the school system there. Out of data analyses and discussions with principals and other leaders in Atlanta, generalizations about desired objectives for practicing principals and criteria pertinent to them could have been evolved. The second approach was more deductive. It involved the retrieval of more generalized knowledge on the objectives of the principalship and performance indicators, the synthesis of this knowledge, and the presentation of it in ways that would allow its usefulness to be tested within the context of specific school systems and in relation to the long-range objectives of the UCEA-Atlanta Project. Clearly, there were advantages and disadvantages to each approach. Given the conditions surrounding the project, however, a decision was made to pursue the more deductive strategy. This choice assumed that a more universal set of concepts could be selected and organized and that the concepts organized would be more lasting and generalizable than those based upon studies in a specific school system. It was also assumed that the broader base of knowledge about educational administration that has been developed in recent decades provided an important source for selecting more universal concepts.

Having chosen the deductive strategy, the first steps were taken to retrieve and synthesize pertinent knowledge. A framework that would facilitate division of labor and the creation of a development team was needed so six different domains of principal behavior were identified. A team of six individuals from five different universities were involved in implementing this first step. The domains resulted from a survey of selected knowledge about educational administration that has evolved during the last decade and from a study of the literature on the needs of principals that might be met through continuing education. The domains, which are treated in the next six chapters, are: administering and improving the instructional program; initiating and responding to change; preparing the organization for effective response; evaluating school processes and products; achieving effective human relations and morale; and making decisions. A seventh individual was added to the team to synthesize ideas presented on the various domains. His ideas are presented in the final chapter.

In their efforts to retrieve and synthesize pertinent knowledge, the authors were asked to describe their domains briefly and to set forth objectives of principal performance within each domain. They were also asked to suggest criteria related to performance and to provide illustrative measures or instruments related to objectives and criteria. A second team—the names are listed in the Preface—was created to assess the work of those charged with retrieving and synthesizing knowledge related to the various domains. No claim is made that the domains encompass all areas of principalship performance. In assessing the domains, however, the authors agreed that the six areas originally chosen should encompass almost all, if not all, significant principal behavior. Suggestions were made for additional domains as, for example, conflict management. It was decided, however, that the topics suggested could be encompassed in the original domains.

It should also be made clear that the domains are not discrete. Since the behavior of principals is expressed as a whole and cannot be broken into absolutely separate categories, there seems to be no easy solution to this problem. Readers should recognize that there is some duplication in the concepts presented in different domains. It is hoped that this will prove to be constructive since the concepts are ordered and presented in different frameworks.

A range of concepts and instruments is presented in the various chapters. These concepts and instruments offer both schools and institutions of higher education many and varied options from which to select. As has already been implied, uses made of the concepts on university campuses will be different from those made by leaders in school systems or other educational institutions. Most institutions, if interested, should find some concepts or instruments pertinent to their objectives. No institution will be able to use all the concepts and instruments immediately. This is true in part because the concepts presented in the various domains have not yet been systematically and fully tested within the context of administrative practice. Thus, a major challenge to prospective users is the further testing, refinement, and development of these concepts and instruments.

POTENTIAL USES OF THE MONOGRAPH

The chapters that follow, then, represent the *first* step in the direction of achieving longer-range objectives. Even though most of the concepts and instruments have not as yet been systematically tested for staff development purposes in specific school systems or program design purposes in universities, there is reason to believe they have a number of potential uses.

Staff Development in School Systems

School leaders are increasingly coming to recognize that the effective improvement of education in school systems cannot be brought about without continuing education programs for personnel responsible for improvement activities. Larger school districts are employing personnel with specific responsibilities for designing and coordinating continuing education programs. These programs are designed to serve the needs of personnel and the goals of school systems. We can safely predict that staff development activities in school systems will continue to increase.

For school systems interested in updating or designing continuing education programs for principals, the concepts and instruments presented in this monograph will require a number of decisions. The first of these has to do with the scope of staff development activities to be implemented. It is possible that a school system would want to limit immediate efforts in continuing education programs for principals to concepts and instruments in one domain, as, for example, "Administering and Improving Instructional Programs," or "Preparing the Organization for Effective Response." Another alternative would be to select more than one domain and to develop a program for principals that cuts across the chosen domains. Finally, there would be the possibility of staging a continuing education program over time in which one domain would be treated, then a second, a third, and so on. A decision made by a school system concerning the scope and content of a program for principals would undoubtedly be related to the resources available and its commitment to staff improvement. In any case, the continuing education needs of all principals should be assessed regularly and opportunities for meeting identified needs should be provided.

Another decision has to do with whether continuing education programs should be differentiated according to the interests of selected groups of principals in a school system or whether they should be oriented toward all principals in the system. In the former case, for example, continuing education experiences might be designed for one group of principals primarily interested in one domain of behavior, for another group they might be related to a second domain, and so on. In the latter case, all principals involved would experience similar programs, although the learning for individuals would vary. A related question has to do with whether or not some principals might design their own learning experiences in their own settings and with their own staffs. In such cases they would adapt concepts and instruments to purposes defined by them and their staffs in contrast to purposes defined more generally for principals in a number of schools.

Efforts to initiate a continuing education program for principals using the concepts and instruments presented in the following chapters could also be addressed in different ways. One way would be to ask leading principals themselves to study the concepts and instruments presented in the various domains and to make judgments about their potential relevance to continuing education programs. Another approach would be to bring together principals as a group, to discuss with them the continuing education needs they perceive as most significant, and then to determine the degree to which the concepts and instruments presented in the various chapters would have judged value for the design of learning experiences. Still a third approach would be to have selected individuals in school systems or institutions of higher education orally present information on the concepts and instruments described in one or more of the chapters to groups of principals, suggesting how these might be used for continuing education purposes. Thereafter, decisions could be made with principals about the scope and content of any continuing education program to be undertaken.

School systems would also have the option of making decisions about scope and content of programs using their own personnel entirely without calling upon external assistance. This might involve, for example, officers of principals' associations and personnel in the central office of school systems interested in and responsible for continuing education. A second alternative would be to involve those from institutions of higher education who are competent in given domains and have expert understanding of concepts in these domains. Those who understand the concepts thoroughly and who have had experience in using the instruments might well suggest a greater number of outcomes and a greater variety of ways for using them.

Should continuing education experiences be conducted within school systems, or should they be held in settings external to practice? Should they involve simulated situations, real situations, or a combination of the two? Should they be short-range or long-range in character, sporadic or continuous? Such questions suggest additional issues which those concerned with the design of specific instructional strategies will face. Financial resources, available expertise, pertinent instructional materials, usable instruments for feedback, motivation of principals, and school board policies will be among the variables that will influence choices particular school systems make with regard to such questions.

Uses in Universities

The concepts presented can also be used by those in institutions of higher education interested in improving instruction or the design of programs for educational administrators. The concepts and instruments, in other words, can provide content for practicing or prospective principals already enrolled in resident or continuing education programs; they can provide opportunities for assessing existing programs for principals and for offering bases for updating or redesigning these programs. They can, in addition, guide internship and other field experience activities.

The various objectives of principal behavior set forth in these chapters and concepts and instruments associated with them can be used, along with other data and concepts, to examine which competencies should be developed in preparatory programs.[6] Questions similar to those faced by personnel designing continuing education experiences for principals in school systems will be faced by those concerned with the design of resident programs. Should design encompass, for example, a few or all components of a program? To what extent should the task of redesign be taken on totally by an institution with external help and to what extent should resource personnel be made available? What instructional strategies should be emphasized in approaching the task?

The concepts and instruments presented in the papers might be used for development purposes other than program design. For example, the concepts might be used to develop needed instructional materials related to the understandings or skills identified during program design. This use would involve first a search to determine what materials related to specified objectives were already available. Then a determination could be made of what needed to be developed. After such decisions were made, appropriate development work could be done. An institution might decide to develop a number of modules, over time, in a sequential fashion. A group of institutions could decide to develop a range of modules through cooperative efforts in a shorter time period.

Still another of the myriad possibilities for using the concepts involves research. Research might be directed at administrator learning, having to do with stated objectives of principal behavior, for example, or it might be directed at performance criteria related to selected objectives, the measurement of behavior, the validation of instruments, or many other areas of inquiry.

The two somewhat independent but related interests of UCEA and Atlanta became joined in the UCEA-Atlanta Project. The Atlanta interest was centered in more effective staff development experiences for principals; the UCEA interest in more effective approaches to applying knowledge to administrative practice.

Four long-range objectives have guided the work of the project to this point and four action guidelines have shaped a general strategy for pursuing objectives. The first stage in the pursuit of the objectives was to select concepts particularly pertinent to the performance of principals from the wide range of knowledge bearing upon educational administration that has evolved during the last decade. Selected knowledge was organized in relation to six domains of principal behavior. Both concepts related to performance and instruments for gathering data on performance were presented.

It should be emphasized that only the first step has been made to achieve objectives of the UCEA-Atlanta Project. Those associated with the project believe, however, that the concepts and instruments achieved can be of general use to leaders in school systems and institutions of higher education interested in training, development, or research, and several potential uses of the concepts and instruments have been identified and briefly delineated.

Perhaps of even greater significance has been the model developed to produce the concepts and instruments. This model resulted from the need to attain more fruitful cooperation between university and school system personnel, and, at the same time, to apply knowledge more effectively to the problems faced and the needs experienced by school leaders. The model also provides new ways to relate major urban school systems with selected universities throughout the nation and to involve leaders in a major development task. Such arrangements should continue to have utility and significance. They will be applied in other contexts, and they will be further refined and improved through use.

NOTES

1. For core concepts in these disciplines related to educational administration, see Jack Culbertson et al., *Social Science Content for Preparing Educational Administrators* (Columbus, Ohio: Merrill Book Company, 1973), chs. 3, 7.

2. See, for example, Robin Farquhar, "Results of a Questionnaire Study," in Jack Culbertson et al., *Preparing Educational Leaders for the Seventies* (Columbus, Ohio: University Council for Educational Administration, 1969), ch. 11.

3. See the following references: James E. Bruno, *The Preparation of School Administrators in Quantitative Analysis* (Columbus, Ohio: University Council for Educational Administration, 1972); Irwin Miklos, *Training-in-Common for Educational, Business and Public Administrators* (Columbus, Ohio: University Council for Educational Administration, 1972); Robin Farquhar and Philip Piele, *Preparing Educational Leaders: A Review of Recent Literature* (Columbus, Ohio: University Council for Educational Administration, 1972).

4. See Keith Goldhammer et al., *Issues and Problems in Contemporary Educational Administration* (Eugene, Ore.: Center for the Advanced Study of Educational Administration, University of Oregon, 1967); Culbertson et al., *Preparing Educational Leaders*, chs. 2, 7.

5. See, for example, E. G. Bogue, "Disposable Organizations," *Phi Delta Kappan*, 53 (No. 2, October 1971), 94-96.

6. Other references that might prove helpful in examining competencies would include the following: National Association of Secondary School Principals, *Pre-service and Continuing Education: Where Will They Find It?* (Washington, D. C.: the Association, 1972); Culbertson et al., *Preparing Educational Leaders*; Keith Goldhammer et al., *Elementary Principals and Their Schools*

(Eugene, Ore.: Center for the Advanced Study of Educational Administration, University of Oregon, 1971); Kenneth McIntyre (ed.), *The Principalship of the 1970's* (Austin, Tex.: Bureau of Laboratory Schools, University of Texas, 1971); Farquhar and Piele, *Preparing Educational Leaders.* Some of the limitations to the competency or behavioral objective approach are described in the following: Philip G. Smith, "On the Logic of Behavioral Objectives," *Phi Delta Kappan,* 53 (No. 7, March 1972), 429-431; W. James Popham, "Objectives '72," *Phi Delta Kappan,* 53 (No. 7, March 1972), 432-435.

TWO

INITIATING AND RESPONDING TO SOCIAL CHANGE

James F. Small

THE NATURE AND SOURCES OF
SOCIAL CHANGE PRESSURES

The role of the school principal in initiating and responding to change could theoretically include the total spectrum of change in the school: administrative and procedural, curricular, extracurricular, guidance, regulatory, disciplinary, and other aspects. This chapter focuses on those areas in which major social changes have impinged upon the school, creating a need for new skills on the part of the principal in dealing with change situations and raising new questions as to the appropriate goals and values from which a principal's behavior should stem.

Although reverberations from major social changes affect the total spectrum of school operations, the principal's role in certain kinds of social change situations involves handling special problems that make these situations different from the normal range of operational change. Adding a course to the high school curriculum, for instance,

Professor Max Birnbaum, Director of the Boston University Human Relations Laboratory, contributed to the development of the concepts on which this chapter is based.

may be a routine matter when the course is offered in response to the interests of a racially mixed group of advanced students who have previously tested out the willingness of a given English teacher to teach a course in humanities as an elective. It may pose a somewhat different problem when a group of black students or persons representing a group in the black community demand the addition of Swahili to the curriculum if a sizable group of white parents is actively organized to oppose such a change.

Social change situations currently of major concern to schools include:

1. the variety of problems stemming from integration;
2. the increasing concern with the "disadvantaged" and the variety of instructional or behavioral problems related to the socioeconomic factor;
3. changes in the nature of authority in our society and consequent effects upon relationships critical to the school context, for example, teacher-student, teacher-principal, or student-parent relationships.

Any effort to develop guidelines in order to examine the principal's role in dealing with such changes must first determine what change situations and resultant problems are most prominent in a particular school system, or even a particular school. Student militancy, racial polarization, the resurgence of ethnicity, fractionalization within a given racial or ethnic constituency, conflicts around the issue of community control, women's rights issues—any of these general trends of social change may pose problems for a given principal, depending upon the particular composition and history of the constituencies that make up his school. Social change trends, in constant flux and often interwoven, can only be effectively measured if the structure and format of measurement efforts build in sufficient flexibility to ensure that the content areas to be dealt with can vary with the circumstances. Otherwise, instruments and procedures can rapidly become obsolete. Means of obtaining input from a given school and its principal in order to identify and assess specific change problems will be considered later.

One way of categorizing the range of such changes is to identify the multiple sources of impetus for change within a school situation:

1. changes stemming from outside the school system—legal changes

such as court-ordered bussing or societal changes such as the population shift from cities to suburbs to exurbs;

2. changes originating from the central office or area office of the school district—experimental instructional programs or district-wide policy changes;

3. changes initiated by the principal—efforts at involving the faculty in enforcement of discipline in the halls, pressuring the central office for greater discriminatory power in handling suspensions and expulsions;

4. changes stemming from the teachers—faculty pressure for a reduction of nonteaching duties, pressure for a greater voice in decision making;

5. changes sought by students—curriculum changes, modification of school rules and regulations regarding student behavior, a greater voice in decision making, a voice in teacher selection and evaluation;

6. pressure from parents for changes in such areas as classification or promotional procedures for students, curriculum, personnel (addition of specialists);

7. pressure from community groups—racial, ethnic, or religious—seeking changes in school life which they would see as benefiting their children: black history courses added to curriculum, accountability of schools to the community.[1]

The principal's role is further complicated in situations where change puts him in the middle of a multiplicity of conflicting pressures from these sources. With all of the constituencies of the school becoming increasingly vocal, with conflicts of group interest often present, and with frequent fractionalization within constituencies, pressures upon the line administrator are increased, and the task of carving out an appropriate and effective posture is made more difficult.

For example, what does a principal do when the white and black communities present conflicting demands based on opposite perceptions, blacks feeling that whites have many advantages and feeling that changes to alleviate prejudicial treatment are necessary, whites feeling that blacks are receiving preferential treatment? When teachers feel that their authority has been eroded and discipline needs to be reasserted, while students feel that they are still subject to unnecessary rules, how does the principal, if called into a disciplinary situation, establish guidelines for deciding when the student must change, when the teacher must change, and when the rules must change? How does a principal respond to conflicting pressures from different factions within a constituency, such as parents' groups organized both for and against bussing?

Given this context in which the critical change situations in the school often involve multiple group interests, emotionally charged issues, or conflicting group needs resulting in conflicting pressures on the principal, examination of the principal's role in dealing with change poses a complex problem of measurement. He is only one factor, though a crucial one, in a social system. To accurately measure his performance in context, one must, in effect, assess the status of the system which it is his responsibility to administer. One cannot, however, fall into the trap of assuming that the state of that system is a direct result of his input alone. One must look both at what the principal does and at what happens in the system and be able to distinguish when he is doing the best job possible but factors beyond his control are causing the system to function poorly, or when he is making many mistakes but the system is operating relatively smoothly in spite of him. This may mean that at least some minimal profile of the changes, issues, and group concerns in the school is a necessary background against which any assessment of the principal's role in initiating and responding to change must be understood.

ROLE OPTIONS FOR THE PRINCIPAL

The principal may perform a number of optional roles related to change. Choice of the most appropriate or effective role is often a matter of value judgment, either the principal's personal value judgment or the principal's perception of what organizational values dictate. His objectives may differ according to the role he is playing:

1. *Initiator.* The principal makes changes according to his perception of the need and asks the appropriate constituencies to implement them. He may, in this instance, be involved in interpreting the nature of the change and the rationale for the change.

2. *Stimulator.* The principal recognizes a problem area as one requiring that the decision to change must come from elsewhere than himself and provides the opportunity for the appropriate constituencies to develop recommendations as to what changes are necessary.

3. *Reactor.* The principal is the recipient of a request from teachers, students, or others for a change that is within his sphere of authority, and he responds directly to the situation.

4. *Implementor.* The principal is required to implement changes decided upon by central administration. This may require direct action, interpretation to others, or involvement of constituent groups.

5. *Conduit.* The principal receives requests from above or below in the hierarchy or from parent or community groups for a change that he perceives as not falling within his sphere of authority. He may then play an intermediary role and seek to connect those requesting change with the appropriate party.

6. *Orchestrator-Mediator.* In complex situations involving multiple and conflicting pressures for change from different groups, the principal may seek to create the context in which change can be negotiated among the parties concerned. In this case he is attempting to achieve collaboration of those whose mutual understanding of and commitment to the proposed change would be necessary if it is to be implemented. The principal's goal is to perform a bridging function.

7. *Persuader or Dissuader.* When the principal feels that proposed change is inappropriate, untimely, unnecessary, or destructive, he may play the role of attempting to persuade those proposing change not to push for the change they have proposed, to push for something else, or to change the timing of their efforts.

8. *Advocate.* When the principal feels that pressure for change is appropriate and necessary, he may choose to support those pushing for the change and join them in attempting to bring the change about.

9. *Ombudsman.* The principal, without himself becoming an advocate, voices the concerns of any group whose point of view might otherwise not be given adequate consideration. He may, for instance, speak for students or faculty in administrative decision-making contexts where these groups do not have a direct voice but where their interests need to be considered if realistic decisions are to be made.

10. *Nonactor.* When the principal feels that requests for change are intended only to be provocative or for any reason could best be handled by "benign neglect," he may choose to make only minimal response to the change proposal and not actively pursue any of the above roles.

These roles are not mutually exclusive, and one of the major determinants of the effectiveness of principal behavior with respect to change is the principal's ability to manage the multiple roles he must play in the change process and to fashion a role appropriate to the situation. For example, in measuring principal performance one would want to know whether a principal reacts with inaction or presents himself as a conduit in situations which require active leadership on his part? Does he act as an advocate or initiator in situations which require a mediational role? How effectively does he orchestrate or stimulate participation of students, teachers, parents, and others in situations where their involvement is necessary to the implementation of change? Is there any pattern to the situations in which the principal develops an appropriate role regarding change and those with which he has difficulty?

The question of what role is "appropriate" in what situation depends upon the superordinate goals and values out of which the principal acts, whether consciously or unconsciously. These may be personal goals and values, or they may be organizational. Organizational values may be explicit (a clearly stated policy statement) or implicit (communicated informally or implied through the patterns of reward and punishment incurred by principal behavior). Since social change, by its nature, often stems from needs and concerns which existing procedural and policy-making structures have not proved sufficient to handle, the principal must often rely heavily on his own experience or native wit in situations where organizational goals are undefined, vaguely defined, inapplicable, in a state of flux, or simply unworkable. Faced with a conflict situation, for instance, he must take whatever action he deems necessary to resolve it in a fashion consistent with his perception of the mandate of his job. Unless it is a question of a principal's violating a clearly defined school system policy, a major problem in assessing his performance becomes that of developing criteria to judge the appropriateness of his goals as well as the effectiveness of his actions in achieving them. If a school system wishes to develop performance criteria for its principals in relation to their handling of social change problems, it must first take a hard look at what the change problems are, what its principals are doing about them, and what the school system feels they should be doing.

It would be inappropriate for me to presume to establish values for a school system, and it would be foolhardy to specify exactly what role a principal should play in a given situation. It might, however, be worthwhile to clarify my general view as to what kinds of situations generally require what kinds of roles. The caveat should, of course, be entered that the individual personality and administrative style of the principal cannot be ignored. There is nothing inherently good or bad in any of the ten change roles itemized above. It may well be that, given the same situation, one principal could effectively initiate change and persuade his faculty to implement it, while another principal might solve the same problem by stimulating his faculty to develop its own solution to the problem. Indeed, one principal's style may be so heavily "charismatic" that he would find it difficult to function as a stimulator, while another principal might find aggressive individual initiative uncomfortable. Similarly, a faculty might accept behavior from one principal which it would not accept from another. One cannot expect individuals to be able to switch roles as easily as changing clothes. One can, however, make some generalizations as to what kinds of roles are most appropriate in what kinds of change situations. From such generalizations a picture can be developed of what, ideally, the principal's role vis-à-vis social change requires and what, realistically, a school system may expect from its principals.

The kinds of social change alluded to above—integration, education of the "disadvantaged," changes in the nature of authority, and so forth—lend themselves to the development of group conflict situations such as black-white, high socioeconomic-low socioeconomic, and teacher-student conflicts, where the principal is frequently caught "in the middle." His mandate involves ensuring that members of all racial, ethnic, religious, and socioeconomic groups receive an education. For this to occur, he must have the collaboration of faculty, students, parents, and the community in agreeing to common ground rules (course of study, disciplinary rules) and to special programs for different exceptional groups (remedial programs for the disadvantaged, special programs for the exceptionally capable student).

In light of current trends toward racial and ethnic group consciousness, questioning of traditional authority, and pressing for community control and greater student participation in decisions about school life, the principal's role has become increasingly important, increasingly visible, and subject to public criticism in areas where real or perceived conflicts of group interests are involved. It is in precisely these areas, where the traditional authority of the principal has been so eroded, that some of the roles that would have been accepted as standard operating procedure in the past are no longer viable. It is not necessary to argue whether traditional roles are ideologically desirable; it is only necessary to ask whether they are practicable if the principal wishes to ensure adequate order for the educational process to proceed with minimum disruption, equitable allowance for the differing educational needs of groups in a pluralistic society, and a system in which changes can occur through a fair negotiation of differences rather than one in which the status quo is rigidly preserved or in which "anomie" prevails.

If one accepts these as minimal values, serious questions must then be raised as to the appropriateness of the initiator, reactor, implementor, conduit, nonactor, and advocate roles in group conflict situations. Each of these roles has certain problems built into it when ostensible or tacit conflict among groups is involved.

If the principal as initiator relies upon his own perception of the needed change and takes the initiative (by decree) in making the change, he remains a potential scapegoat. Whatever change is made remains his own "psychological property." Any challenge to it is a challenge to his personal judgment, and he is liable to respond to it as such. If the change is perceived as favoring one group as opposed to another, he will be seen as favoring that group or as yielding to their pressures. Unless he has sought input from all constituencies involved, his perception of the need may be inaccurate. Although he is liable to receive full credit for a "good" decision, he may also receive full blame for a "bad" one. Even when his initiation of the change proves to be a wise choice, there may be less sense of satisfaction among those who favored the change than there would have been if they had had a hand in fashioning it themselves and it was their own "psychological property." Whereas any challenge to a collaboratively planned change affects all concerned, it is easier for any single group to "write off" a decreed change as one man's product. If, as is often the case, a principal's leadership and authority is subject to challenge from a variety of quarters and he responds by a heightened effort to reassert that authority in the face of considerable resistance, his credibility as a leader is vulnerable. He must ask himself what he can do if a significant number of persons refuse to follow his lead. Only when he is reasonably sure that he is representing the interests or an acceptable compromise of the interests of all or nearly all significant factions can the principal take a unilateral initiative in making changes to resolve group conflicts. It is certainly not advisable, where action is required, that he "run scared"; nonetheless, he must be sure of the wisdom of his initiative. Otherwise he had better consider another of the active options. (It should be noted that terms such as "good," "bad," and "wise" in reference to a given decision to make a change are meant in this context to be descriptive of the practicability of the change, which depends upon the acceptance or rejection of the change by those whose cooperation is necessary for its implementation.) We are concerned here with developing general guidelines for the resolution of group conflicts, not with a value judgment as to the merit of the changes with which they are concerned. It is quite possible that there are times when a principal may decide that a given change is absolutely necessary, and he estimates that, although it is unpopular, once he has advanced it it will be accepted. He may, at times, decide that it must be attempted even if it does not work. The point is that, as a general rule, unilateral initiative by the principal in group conflict situations involves a sufficient number of pitfalls to make it seldom the role of choice. If a principal is accustomed to making changes by decree, even if this approach appears to be working effectively, he is vulnerable if a major group conflict becomes centered around a given change issue.

Similar caution must be applied to the role of reactor, in which the principal takes action in response to a request for change from others. Although a perfectly legitimate role, this again may not be the role of choice in a group-conflict situation where response to one group's desires may be seen by others as favoritism or as yielding to pressure, particularly if the change issue is seen as one which affects all, not just the group which requested it. If the principal grants nearly all requests, he may be seen as weak or fearful, and he will have special difficulty when he receives contradictory requests. If he seldom grants a request, he may be storing up the fuel of discontent which will eventually break out in disruption. Only the most skillful principal, who can establish and interpret fair and just criteria for his positive and negative responses to proposed changes can avoid the pitfalls of the reactor role in situations where conflicts of group interest are present.

The important factor held in common by the initiator and reactor roles, is that they both involve unilateral action by the principal, whether in response to his own perceptions or to the expressed desires of others. In a traditional, "chain of command" model of authority, the appropriateness of this role is consensually understood by all members of the hierarchy. In public schools today it is being severely challenged by nearly all constituencies. Students' rights, teacher militancy, community control, "concerned" parents—these are becoming common phrases in many school systems, and the issues involved do not appear to be abating. Although one could make a value-based argument for the desirability of this changing nature of authority, it is likewise possible to argue that much is being lost as a result of this trend. It is becoming increasingly difficult, however, to deny that traditional roles of authority are becoming more and more difficult to implement in dealing with group conflicts in our schools and that effective roles must be found if these conflicts are to be resolved. From a practical standpoint, those who wish to see some form of order prevail are beginning to find that a reassertion of the traditional authority role does not always work; it may actually make things worse. Although exceptionally capable principals, principals who have a relatively homogeneous community without major group conflicts or principals in whose schools these conflicts remain latent, may be able to continue to run their schools effectively through the exercise of traditional hierarchical authority, many now face situations in which the other parties involved in school life no longer see educators as persons whose authority they must respect but rather as persons who should provide service, for which they can be held accountable.

On the other hand, there are pitfalls at the other end of the spectrum of role options. A principal must be wary of the consequences of presenting himself as a conduit or an implementor or of choosing to be a nonactor. Unless he follows up on what he has relayed to higher administration and keeps those involved informed of the progress of the consideration being given to their concerns, the role of conduit will be seen as merely one of "buck-passing." If he relies too heavily on the implementor role in presenting himself, it will soon be interpreted as a "cop out," especially if the changes for which he is attributing responsibility elsewhere are ones which involve consider-able leeway for interpretation at the local level. Equally apparent is the risk involved in the nonactor role, for if the change requests turn out to be significant ones after all, the principal is culpable for having ignored them.

The role of advocate involves special dynamics, for the principal is not only taking the initiative in reacting to change pressures, he is also, in a sense, joining the camp of those pushing for specific changes. Some would argue that there are instances where this form of leadership is required and any other posture is an avoidance of responsibility. The question may be raised, on the other hand, as to whether advocacy may also undermine the principal's potential lever-age as a mediator when there are conflicting factions unable to agree upon an issue of change in the school. As the principal's role be-comes increasingly "politicized" by the social controversies being acted out in the school arena, he will frequently be forced to take sides or to carve out a professional role somewhere between the op-posing factions. Although it is important that the principal not deny his own opinions, it may still be necessary in certain circumstances that he distinguish personal opinion from professional role. The major argument for this distinction in a context of conflict among groups is simply: "If the school principal does not play some sort of a 'middle' role in dealing with diverse and conflicting factions, who will?" And, if no one plays such a role in the school, can the educa-tional process be maintained?

Several of the roles listed earlier may offer valuable options to the principal who is able to identify situations which call for a "man in the middle" role. These include ombudsman, persuader-dissuader, stimulator, and orchestrator-mediator.

As ombudsman, for instance, a principal would handle pressures for changes that are beyond his authority by assuming an active role in presenting the concerns to the appropriate persons. Rather than acting as a disinterested party, merely passing on information (con-duit), or taking a strong personal position on the matter (advocate), the principal would make an effort at interpreting the reasons for the change pressure and the feelings of those pressing for the change as well as the dynamics of the situation and the potential options for response. He would, in effect, be actively bridging the gap between those pushing for change and those with the authority to respond to that push.

As persuader-dissuader he might bridge the gap in the opposite direction, interpreting the larger organizational situation to any given group advocating change. This could mean lending his counsel as to timing or strategy for getting an issue considered, or it could mean attempting to redirect the efforts at change by suggesting a more productive short-range route to a long-range goal. It involves an active effort to work with a given group, to inform them of the constraints on change, the appropriate avenues for seeking change and the possible directions toward which the principal would or would not be willing to help them push, and, if not, the reasons why. The important distinction here is that the principal deals as openly as possible with the realities of the situation, including his own opinions and perceptions as well as those of all groups involved, rather than presenting himself as a "reactor" or "nonactor," simply listening to all that a group has to say and then acting in whatever fashion he sees fit or choosing not to act. He does not in any way relinquish his own ultimate responsibility and authority, but he accepts counsel from those who offer it and informs them of the other factors he must consider.

As a stimulator, the principal does not wait for others to approach him with change requests or demands. He keeps a weather eye open for signs of problems that may lead to a need for change and attempts to stimulate those whose interests are involved to become active in generating plans for change. He thus avoids the pitfalls of unilaterally initiating the change himself or of waiting until others push in a given direction to which he must say yes or no. He also creates a situation in which change has a much better chance of being successfully implemented since it evolves from the affected parties acting in concert with administrative encouragement. Rather than attempting to head off the storm by pre-emptive action or allowing discontent to mount to a potentially disruptive level, the principal attempts to develop a norm, as well as appropriate structures and procedures, to encourage faculty, students, and others to become involved in continual reassessment of the need for change, collaborative planning for change, and implementation of change plans. This approach involves a recognition that social change is an inevitable and, at least for the present, accelerating process. Often it can neither be avoided nor reversed, but it can be managed.

As an orchestrator-mediator the principal attempts to coordinate the diverse and often conflicting needs of the constituencies that participate in school life. In group conflict situations he plays a third-party role, whether arbitrating conflict or organizing and presiding over efforts at negotiation of differences. The important insight on the principal's part is recognition that schools, although traditionally hierarchial in authority structure, have been able to operate in this fashion only through the consent of parents, community, students, and others. At the present time, even the most traditional structures —the army, the church, the police—are hard pressed to maintain this mode of operation without significant changes. Public schools are especially vulnerable to the effects of social change because of their central role in the lives of the total citizenry, their great importance to the social and financial success of every student, the high personal investment which parents, on the whole, have in the success or failure of their children, and historical circumstance, which has made the public school the battleground for resolution of our major societal ills (racial conflicts, youth-age conflicts, and so forth). At a time when major industries such as the automobile industry are recognizing the necessity for experimentation with collaborative systems of management in a situation where the powerful sanction of hiring and firing (albeit mollified by the power of unions) is in the hands of management, how can a principal expect to deal with a social system such as the school without some similar effort at developing a wide range of participation? Aside from the question of the desirability of the traditional authority role, it is highly questionable whether principals have sufficient clout or sanctions at their disposal to manage group conflicts effectively through the exercise of power. If this proves true, some of the roles described above may provide useful alternatives.

The "ideal" principal, from the point of view of ability to deal effectively with social change, would be a person who is able to recognize those conflict situations which require a "third-party" role and respond appropriately, despite the fact that he may frequently play a variety of other roles in handling other administrative duties. Although values and personal style may have an impact on the ease with which he can operate in a "third-party" role, this is not to say that a principal must be ideologically committed to the universal use of a collaborative approach to change problems; even if it were desirable, it might not be feasible. It can be said that he must be able to recognize when major sociopolitical issues are involved and be willing, if only to survive in his job, to try to carve out some kind of "middle" role for himself rather than resorting to an ineffectual edict or avoiding the situation. Since principals are recruited from the human race, this willingness to try to evolve a new role is as much as anyone can realistically expect from a person being forced to deal on a daily basis with the effects of a multitude of social issues, many of which are substantially beyond his control.

A final word of caution about the above generalizations: there will always be principals who appear to handle a variety of situations very effectively while violating every guideline as to what "should" be the role of choice. One cannot, however, fall into the trap of developing performance criteria for the exceptional principal. The guidelines discussed above are based on the assumption that the purpose in developing criteria is to develop a model that can be applied to more than just the exceptionally talented. One advantage of the "third-party" roles described is that they have the potential for enabling a principal to enlist the talents of others in seeking solutions to change problems. Hence a principal who is an effective orchestrator-mediator, stimulator, ombudsman, or persuader-dissuader and can appropriately spread the burden which he bears rather than attempt to carry the whole weight on his own shoulders may well increase his chances to solve problems.

THE ASSESSMENT OF PRINCIPAL PERFORMANCE

Application of performance criteria may be approached in at least three different ways depending upon how a school system answers the question posed earlier as to whose values are to be applied in assessing performance. A school system may define its own values and attempt to measure the degree to which a principal implements them; it may adopt criteria generated by a third party (my theory of appropriate role behavior in group-conflict situations) and attempt to measure the degree to which principals behave in this manner; it may attempt to determine what principals see as their goals and whether they are effective by their own standards. If the school system wishes the assessment process to be a fruitful endeavor for the principals involved as well as for the system, it may be highly desirable to begin with the third approach. Once a system knows what its principals are trying to do and what they are doing, it can then begin to answer the question of what they "ought" to do. This approach has the advantage of providing basic descriptive data, rather than attempting to test predetermined hypotheses. It is essentially a clinical research approach with a potential for theory building, rather than a classical theory-testing approach. Of critical importance here is the recognition that the principal's role in dealing with social change is a relatively uncharted area which requires exploration; it is not an area of principal behavior for which clear standards exist.

Furthermore, inasmuch as the medium is the "message" there is an immensely important by-product of this approach, apart from any theoretical considerations. This methodology carries a message to principals: the school system wants to learn about their problems in order to help them. The system addresses itself to the problems of the job as perceived by the principal and others in the school as a starting point. It does not evaluate them solely by criteria generated in the central or area office or in the university. As a point of practical strategy alone, this may well make the difference as to whether useful and valid data will be obtained.

This strategy also provides a means of evolving a focus which will define the critical areas in which the principal's role requires reexamination. The boundaries of the domain of change are wide. It would be most fruitful if assessment focused on those areas which are seen as most crucial to school life and those areas which pose new problems for the principal. The specific kinds of changes to be explored must be generated from within the school system. A substantial input from the principals as to their perception of the change problems should be sought. Principals, in a sense, know the change problems best since they face them every day.

A principal's goals in relation to change may vary according to the role he chooses to play; however, one cannot assume that this choice is always a conscious one. The school system may first want to find out whether principals are aware of the postures they are taking before questioning how appropriate or effective such postures are. This may well mean that an open-ended or projective approach to measurement should be incorporated into the initial stages of any effort to develop criteria for performance. The basic idea would be to develop a profile of the principal's perception and understanding of social change in his school, as well as of his behavior in dealing with such changes.

It must be remembered, however, that the principal's job performance can only be measured by looking at the functioning of his school and all the constituencies involved in school life. Yet the principal cannot be credited or blamed as the sole determining factor of the functioning of a school. His input is pivotal, but it is not the only input. To develop a profile of principal performance, one would need to look at the principal's role in relationship to teachers, community, students, parents, and others and, in effect, to develop a profile of the functioning of the school. If the school system accepts this posture, it should be made clear to principals since this might alleviate some of the natural concerns of those being evaluated.

If a profile of school functioning is necessary in order to assess principal performance, it might be desirable to put any measurement effort in the context not simply of an assessment of the principal, but of an effort to help principals assess the way their schools are functioning and what they can do about it, building in feedback of the data generated to the principal. It is assumed here that measurement could provide valuable learning for the principal as well as for the school system concerning the need principals have for supportive services. Such an assessment process might then become a periodic review process useful to all parties involved.

Given these assumptions and their implications for the strategy of approaching measurement, one must determine what kinds of data need to be gathered, what criteria should be applied in inferring principal performance from the data, and what procedures can be employed in utilizing the data to help resolve the problems of the school.

It is particularly important in dealing with the domain of change that principals be involved collaboratively in planning the assessment process if useful and valid data are to be gathered. Interpretation of the purpose of the enterprise to faculty or anyone else involved is similarly critical if a climate is to be created which will enable the assessment to tap perceptions accurately. If there is any doubt as to the motives for collecting information or the use to which it will be put, a number of confounding factors could be elicited. Guardedness lest what faculty have said should come back to haunt them, defensiveness on the part of the principal, denial of problems, or utilization of this process as an opportunity to press "political" concerns are all most likely to occur in situations where there are the most problems and, consequently, where there is the greatest need for help.

Safeguards must be built in to ensure that the assessment is as fair, accurate, unbiased, and beneficial as possible and that it is perceived as such by those in the school. Several strategies can help ensure this:

1. Prior interpretation of the assessment and an orientation of those to be involved on a face-to-face basis are important.

2. A team can carry out the assessment in situations where interview or observation is involved and subjective judgments are a factor. The assessment team could include central or area office staff, or a combination of the two.

3. Feedback of data to the principal and encouragement of follow-up on concerns identified by himself and others in the school help.

4. Follow-up by the school system on needs identified, such as in-service training, other supportive services, and administrative follow-up is useful.

5. When tapping subjective areas (faculty or principal's perceptions of principal's role or faculty and principal's perceptions of desirable changes), efforts must be made to focus on specific behaviors observed or advocated rather than on global judgments. For instance, one does not ask a faculty member whether his feeling about the principal's leadership in dealing with change pressures from students is positive or negative. One asks what actions he is aware of that the principal has taken in specific situations; what results these actions appear to him to have had; in what policy areas (hall discipline, drugs, or others) he is clear as to his own responsibilities, and in what areas he is unclear; what mechanisms there are for voicing his own concerns or for seeking clarification of his responsibilities.

6. Assessment must also focus on existing mechanisms for change, awareness of these mechanisms, effectiveness of the mechanisms, areas in which such mechanisms need to be developed, whether existing mechanisms involve truly representative participation, and ways in which existing mechanisms can be improved or supplemented. For instance, rather than asking a principal to assess the general status of school-community relations, one asks what organized structure exists for handling parental pressures for change, what kinds of specific pressures he has dealt with recently or is currently dealing with, what actions he has taken, and so forth.

7. Assessment should focus wherever possible on "case studies" in attempting to derive a picture of how change situations are handled by the principal and how mechanisms for change are functioning in

the school. People can thus refer concretely to what happened, to what could be done in similar circumstances in the future or to what could be done to prevent similar problems from developing in the future.

8. In order to do this effectively, it must be clear that this is a standard procedure being used to provide a basis for helping principals with change problems currently hitting most of the schools in the country. It is not based on an assumption that the principal's actions are suspect and require investigation. It will seek to identify what kinds of actions, mechanisms, and policies work best as well as to identify which have been counterproductive. Although it would probably be of little learning value to explore only examples which are seen as "success" stories by all concerned, it should be clear that there is as much interest in knowing what worked well and why as in knowing what went wrong and why.

9. The profile of a given principal's performance includes input from the various constituencies of the school as well as self-evaluation and the judgments of the school system's evaluation team. It is thus comprehensive and collaborative.

10. Wherever ambiguities or contradictions are found in data generated by questionnaire or other indirect means, face-to-face situations are built in to allow the assessment team to check out such factors.

In view of the logistical problems involved in seeking data from all constituencies in the school, it may be necessary to modify the ideal circumstance which would involve development of a profile that would include data from parents, students, teachers, principal, and community. Assuming that the initial assessment process needs to be brief enough to be administratively feasible but valid enough to be of practical use, it might be best to focus primarily on the principal himself and the faculty as the group with whom he is most directly concerned.

Assuming this focus, the following assessment sequence would be one example of a possible approach to measurement:

1. *Orientation for principals.* This could be done by the team with the individual principal, or in a group meeting where feasible. A group orientation for high school or junior high school principals, for example, might be most feasible as well as desirable, both in terms of numbers in a large system and in terms of the fact that change issues

are often most severe at this level, due to the additional complexities resulting from the age factor.

2. *Orientation of the faculty and faculty questionnaire.* Orientation might be done in conjunction with the initial data gathering from the faculty in the form of a questionnaire designed to elicit: (a) general indexes of the school climate, (b) specific data on change issues, (c) specific data on change mechanisms, (d) specific data on faculty perceptions of principal behavior. (See Appendix A for sample questions.)

3. *Principal questionnaire.* This questionnaire would focus on: (a) principal's perception of school climate, (b) principal's perception of change issues, (c) specific data on change mechanisms, (d) principal's description of his own behavior including the values, goals, and strategies on the basis of which he operates, as well as his perception of organizational values, goals, and expectations. (See Appendix B for sample questions.)

4. *Assessment conference of team and principal.* This would include: (a) feedback of data gathered from the faculty to the principal, (b) comparison of faculty and principal data, (c) exploration of areas which appear to be unclear or to involve contradictory data.

5. *Checking out data with resource groups.* Groups would be interviewed by the team in order to check out their perceptions regarding change issues agreed upon by the principal and the team as needing further exploration as well as consideration of mechanisms for input from these groups. These groups could include parents, students, and community groups, and they should insofar as possible be representative samples of these populations. Constituent groups should be interviewed separately, twelve to fifteen persons at a time.

6. *Summarizing of data by the team and rating of principal.* Performance must be judged according to criteria. (See Appendix C for sample criteria.)

7. *Feedback of data to the principal and consideration of follow-up needs (by the principal and by the school system).*

The foregoing sample assessment sequence is based on the assumption that assessment of current principal performance would be a logical first step. Data gathered through such a process could then form the basis for identifying in-service training needs and other needs for supportive services, and for developing a basis for selection and preservice training of principals. The selection process might well include questionnaire data, a structured interview, and response to written (or, ideally, videotaped) vignettes of change situations derived from the range of data documented by the process for assessing current principal performance. In-service training could include experience focused on exploration of attitudes and values related to social change and the group conflicts involved in change issues, role-play practice at handling change situations; input on strategies of change using concrete examples from the school system's experience; exposure to resource groups (current principals, parents, teachers, students, and so forth). Again, the specific examples and the focuses of training could derive from what is learned in the assessment of current principal performance. The assessment sequence described above would require modifications before it could be implemented.

Time required. The data could be gathered and processed through a series of half-day visits by the team, primarily with the principal. The gathering of faculty data would need to be fitted, ideally, into a regular faculty meeting. Resource group interviews might best be done in a full day, if possible. Since this involves substantial time, some decision would have to be made as to whether the full process is fruitful enough to merit the time commitment. A trial run or two might form the basis for a judgment as to whether the process can be streamlined and improved or if criteria can be established which would call for a shortened version being applied in schools where prior data are available and need not be duplicated.

Flexibility. Some determination as to the kinds of change issues to be focused on across the board and those to be explored only in some cases would have to be made. There may, for instance, be significant differences in the areas one would explore in secondary as opposed to elementary schools. Again, preliminary input from principals would be useful here.

Availability of personnel. A judgment as to the amount of personnel resources available for this project would need to be made. This could influence the feasibility of an assessment in depth versus a more superficial survey.

Data required. If there are needs for specific data or for data in a readily computable form, this may mean that the form of recording would have to be simplified or otherwise modified.

Data on the existence and effectiveness of mechanisms for change and on the principal's behavior in dealing with change situations form the core of the assessment process. Any modification of the process that did not provide some check on perceptions other than those of the principal or some opportunity for a face-to-face probing of issues raised by initial questionnaire data would be vulnerable to questions regarding its validity and its superficiality. Ideally, the process of helping principals deal with social change requires not only measurement, but also a major effort at training, utilizing both external consultants and internal resources. In the social change area, external consultants can play a crucial role since this frequently controversial and confused area strongly requires an objective third party to help a school system develop structures and methods for problem assessment and solution. No third party can, however, have a lasting impact unless provision is made for developing resources within the system to carry on the effort once the consultants have gone. It is from experience with a model of third-party intervention for organizational change (in relation to intraschool and school-community issues) that I have adapted many of the concepts developed in the assessment sequence described above. This intervention model has been developed in working with a number of urban and suburban school systems in an effort to prepare the total system, including the principals, to deal with social change.[2] Although the assessment sequence described above is designed to be carried out primarily through internal resources, I would be remiss not to point out that external consultation can be of considerable value in demonstrating and implementing the procedures required for any such effort. Assessment of social change issues requires a background and a repertoire of skills that may not be immediately available internally, but that can be developed in certain individuals identified as "trainable" for this role on the basis of their interest, personality, and experience.

On the other hand, it must be recognized that many school systems may not have either the internal or external resources to mount a large-scale effort. Such systems may wish to consider an "instrumented" approach to assessment or training. This approach would have to be designed to stimulate principals to become aware of the issues involved in their role vis-à-vis social change and to reconsider their own perceptions and behavioral options. Instruments could be designed either as the basis for developing discussion in an in-service training context, for gathering data on principal behavior in dealing with change issues, or for both. An instrumented approach presumes that there is no expert team, internal or external, to take the principals through the process. At the most, there may be a person required to orient principals to the procedure and to moderate the discussion; at the least, there may simply be written instructions specifying timing, content, and sequence for a self-administering instrument designed for individual or group use. For example, the ten roles described earlier as options for principal behavior with respect to change might be dealt with through a number of instrumented approaches: a self-descriptive questionnaire designed to help a principal identify patterns in his own philosophy or style of behavior in dealing with change;[3] a series of written simulation exercises presenting the principal with a hypothetical change problem and a description of context and requiring a written response which could then be scored according to the roles he employed;[4] a direct reporting questionnaire describing the roles and asking the principal to describe situations in his own experience in which he has played each of the ten roles and to give his opinion as to the appropriateness of roles to situations.

A sequence of instruments should be designed first to stimulate the principals to generate data that represent their perceptions; second, to provide a conceptual framework and procedural guidelines for self-assessment through examination of the data, either individually or preferably through group discussion; and, third, to encourage consideration of the implications of the learnings generated for the principal's job behavior. Such a sequence would provide data which could give the principals an opportunity to re-examine their own job functioning and derive applicable learning, as well as providing data from which the school system could obtain a profile of current problems principals are facing and how they are being handled.[5]

In dealing with emotionally charged social issues, however, it may be necessary, prior to any data gathering, to provide some form of orientation to prepare principals for participation in an examination of change issues. Otherwise basic resistance may interfere with the ability of some principals to accept the format of the questionnaire. Some persons, for instance, are suspicious and resent group labeling; the very thought of describing a situation in terms of group concerns (race, ethnic group, social class, etc.) may offend them because speaking in group terms is perceived as a sign of prejudice. Others are loathe to make generalizations because they see any attempt to generalize as potential stereotyping. The most effective procedure for orientation of the sort required here is a structured group interview, focused on examination of group identifications, including both their importance in the background of the principal and their importance in the intergroup dynamics within school life.[6] Whether this process can be fully instrumented is questionable, but a portion of its purpose may be served by encouraging principals to engage in a structured discussion of their feelings about group identifications prior to proceeding with the instrumented sequence which asks them to describe their school in group terms.[7]

The guidelines suggested here for approaching the problem of developing performance criteria for school principals with respect to their handling of social change must be considered experimental in nature. Although based upon procedures and principles that have proven valuable in other contexts, they are not finished products ready to be transplanted to any given situation; rather, they are guidelines on which to start experimentation. Testing, reorganizing, and modifying of the procedures described and illustrated here should be the next step so that the guidelines can be tailored to fit the needs of a given school system and refined to provide maximum effectiveness.

APPENDIXES

A. SAMPLE QUESTIONS FOR FACULTY QUESTIONNAIRE

1. How would you describe the current status of the relationship between black and white students in your classes?
   - (a) Friendly
   - (b) Cordial
   - (c) Laissez-faire
   - (d) Some tension
   - (e) Latent hostility
   - (f) Open hostility

2. What recent changes or proposed changes are currently a source of actual or potential controversy among racial groups in your school? Describe briefly the nature of conflicting views. E.g., are divisions of opinion within the student body between students and teachers in general, between black students and white teachers, between white students and black teachers, between black students and the principal, etc.?

3. What changes in school rules, policies, or procedures can you identify which you feel are necessary to reduce or avoid the racial tensions described above? Do these changes require action on the part of your principal? If so, what action is desirable?

4. What avenues among those listed below are available to teachers in your school who wish to seek changes?
   (a) Raise question at faculty meeting
   (b) Seek individual interview with principal
   (c) Broach issue through teacher union
   (d) Written communication with principal
   (e) Seek interview for yourself and other interested parties with principal
   (f) Ongoing advisory group of faculty
   (g) Ad hoc faculty committee
   (h) Other

5. Which of the above, if any, have you had occasion to use within the past year? What change was sought? What was the result?

6. In terms of your past experience, how would you rate each of the above in terms of effectiveness as an avenue for influencing or changing the functioning of the school: very effective, sometimes effective, seldom effective, waste of time?

7. Do you have any suggestions for improvement of existing avenues or creation of new mechanisms for teacher input concerning changes in the school?

8. Which of the following best characterize your feeling as to the appropriate role of the principal in relation to changes in school rules?
   (a) Make what changes he sees fit
   (b) Stimulate students and teachers to take an active role in developing recommendations for change
   (c) Take no action unless or until approached by students, teachers, parents, or others
   (d) Create a context in which students, faculty, and others can work out their differences among themselves when controversy exists over a rule

9. Describe a situation in which your principal responded to a controversy, e.g., over a school rule, policy, or procedure. What did he do? What was the result?

10. Referring to the above situation or others, describe a situation involving actual or proposed changes in rules when you felt the principal's actions were very appropriate. Describe a situation in which you felt that different actions would have been better. What actions would have been better and why?

Note: The assessment team will want to obtain comparable data from faculty and principal regarding principal behavior and role so that in later sessions with the principal an effort can be made to sort out agreements, differences of opinion, misperceptions, or other difficulties between faculty and principal. The faculty questionnaire should be anonymous. It is most important to generate an accurate picture of total faculty opinion and perception, rather than to seek individual points of view and to ask people to go on record. There is no assumption here that faculty perceptions of the principal will always be valid, or, for that matter, that a principal will perceive himself accurately at all times. The effort is to gather specific data about these actions, in order to get a picture of the context in which a principal operates. In assessing the appropriateness, for instance, of a principal's action regarding a change situation, it may be critical to know whether he acted in a situation where he had nearly total faculty support, sought collaboration from faculty who felt that he should take the responsibility for the decision himself, acted in a situation where faculty members were split in their opinion, or acted unilaterally in the face of considerable faculty opposition.

B. SAMPLE QUESTIONS FOR PRINCIPAL QUESTIONNAIRE

1. Which among the following statements best describe faculty feeling about their role in discipline at the current time (estimate approximate percentages of faculty to which each statement applies)?
   (a) Willing and able to "run a tight ship"
   (b) Desires to avoid any confrontation with students and ignores situations that should be handled
   (c) Tends to pass problems on to the administration that could be handled in the classroom
   (d) Afraid to discipline black students
   (e) Afraid to discipline white students
   (f) Feels discipline situation is a generally routine function, not posing any major problem
   (g) Feels frustrated at inability to enforce rules due to general defiance of many students

2. What changes in the school rules, policies or procedures are you aware of which are desired by significant portions of the faculty, the student body, parents, community groups? Which of these involve actual or potential conflict among racial, ethnic, or other groups? What groups have conflicting views, e.g., students and teachers as a whole, black students and white teachers, white students and black teachers, black students and the principal, or others?

3. What specific mechanisms are available to each of these groups for pursuing these changes? How effectively are these mechanisms being employed?

4. Describe a situation in the past in which you have dealt with controversy over a proposed change in school rules, policies, or procedures. What did you do in an effort to resolve the situation? What was the result? What other alternatives did you consider and discard and why?

5. What avenues are you currently pursuing in dealing with the change issues described in Question 2, above?

C. SAMPLE CRITERIA FOR RATING OF PRINCIPAL PERFORMANCE

Face-to-face questioning, following up on questionnaire data, could help the team get a clear impression of the qualities in a principal that can best be estimated by inference from flexible questioning rather than from a written question. They might be able to rate the principal utilizing a number of criteria:

1. Awareness of critical factors determining his own role
   A. How well does the principal appear to sort out the multiple roles and loyalties which place conflicting demands upon him in change situations? Is he able to balance his obligations to respond to the needs of students, teachers, parents, and others?
   B. How well does the principal distinguish his personal opinions and feelings from his professional posture? Is he capable of functioning objectively in situations where his personal convictions differ from his professional obligations?
   C. How capable is the principal of developing criteria for conscious decisions as to the appropriate posture to take? Does he tend to respond unconsciously or automatically, or is he able to develop a planned strategy?
   D. How aware is the principal of the factors influencing his perception of the various motives that lead individuals or groups to advocate change? Does he tend to stereotype groups or overindividualize his interpretations of the motivation for change?

2. Diagnostic skills
   A. How well can the principal differentiate dynamics which emanate from different sources?
      a. intrapsychic dynamics (peculiar to the individual)
      b. group dynamics (for instance, within a whole faculty)
      c. interpersonal dynamics (between two individuals)
      d. interface dynamics (among role groups: student-teacher, faculty-administration, etc.)
      e. intergroup dynamics (black-white, Catholic-Protestant, etc.)
      f. social system dynamics (for instance, school-community)
      Does the principal treat all conflicts between black and white students as racial conflicts? On the other hand, does he consistently seek to portray all such conflicts as personal and not racial? Can he differentiate whether disruptive behavior is related to: serving the individual's need for attention, the individual's expression of the group's feelings, a personal conflict between students, a conflict between racial, ethnic, or religious groups, or a function of parental or community influence on the child? Can he help teachers base their responses to problem situations on diagnosis rather than assumption?
   B. What methods for checking out his diagnosis of the change situation has the principal developed? Can he generate and test out multiple hypotheses regarding the dynamics of the situation? Does he have the necessary contacts with all constituencies to do this?

3. Effective action
    A. Can the principal generate alternative interventions for handling change situations?
    B. Can he develop criteria for distinguishing which intervention is most appropriate?
    C. Can he act effectively to influence situations?
    D. How effectively does he create the context in which change can be handled appropriately by the constituencies involved?
    E. Can the principal develop strategies for the nature and timing of his interventions which take into account the forces driving for and restraining change and the current status of the change equilibrium? Does he know when to push for change and when to work on reducing resistance?[8]

4. Effective efforts at influencing the change climate
    A. Has he made efforts to establish a climate in which teachers, students, and others feel free to be open about problems, or do most people feel that they must keep problems out of the principal's view?
    B. Is there a climate in the school which legitimizes differing points of view about change? What model does the principal's behavior provide? Is he seen as always anxious to change, always anxious to preserve the status quo, or wishy-washy? Is he able to play the kind of professional role which does not encourage faculty, students, and parents to see him as acting out of ideology, thereby putting him in a position where his leadership may be acceptable to opposing ideological factions?

5. Establishment of mechanisms for change
    A. Has the principal helped to establish mechanisms for change and for continual re-evaluation of the need for change?
    B. Has the principal involved those who would have to implement significant changes in behavior in the planning or decision making regarding the changes?
    C. Has the principal created mechanisms for involvement of constituent groups in the change process which ensure true representation? Are those who are involved seen as leaders by the major components of the groups they represent?

Note: In comparing data from principal and faculty, the team may then be in a position to rate the principal in terms of the degree of effort he has put into establishing the kind of climate in which change issues can be handled effectively and into establishing the necessary mechanisms for change. It can also estimate the degree of success his efforts have met and the factors involved in bringing about success or failure, such as faculty apathy or enthusiasm or the effectiveness of the model set by the principal and whether it helps bridge differences or adds to divisiveness, whether it produces understanding or misperception of the motives of the principal on the part of faculty, students, or others.

D. THE PRINCIPAL'S ROLE IN DEALING WITH
GROUP PRESSURES FOR CHANGE

Introduction to the Instrument

A variety of social changes have had a significant impact upon public schools in recent years, leading in turn to increased pressures for change from parents, students, teachers, administration, and community groups. The principal's role can become particularly difficult when change is either actually or potentially controversial, and this is especially true when change becomes an issue which brings about polarization along group lines, either among or within school constituencies (black-white, student-faculty, or other groups). The following sequence of questions is designed to provide a format to help a principal assess the change equilibrium in his own school in terms of identifying group desires, assessing the available mechanisms for handling change concerns, and reviewing his own behavior in dealing with the problems that arise in change situations. This instrument is intended to serve two purposes simultaneously: to stimulate the principal to reassess his situation, leading, it is hoped, to potential insights as to ways in which he can be more effective in his own job role; and to generate information about the current status of change problems and the ways in which they are being handled throughout the school system, so that those responsible for in-service training and other supportive services can provide appropriate help to the principal.

The sequence of questions is designed to be answered by an individual principal or by a group of principals. When using this instrument in a group setting, it is suggested that the questionnaire be interrupted periodically (as designated below) for sharing and discussion of data. Group discussion by several principals or individual reflection by a single principal can both be guided by the set of questions which follows each section of the instrument.

Instructions to the Principal

In approaching the questions, do not be concerned about the fact that you are being asked to make generalizations about groups. Just give the best estimation you can. You may assume that your statements need only be true in a significant proportion of cases (say 70 percent) to be valid generalizations. If you wish to make particular note of important exceptions to generalizations you are being asked to make, feel free to do so. Be as honest and thorough as possible in answering the questions. There is no hidden meaning in them. If you are unsure of an answer, you may indicate that fact and give the best answer you can; if you absolutely do not know, you may say so. A major purpose of the questionnaire is to provide you with an opportunity to examine your own perceptions (in the group setting you will also be able to compare perceptions with other principals). Do not allow yourself to be concerned about how others might respond to your answers or what answers might be expected. There are no right or wrong answers. Questions are designed to enable you to give a profile of your own school and your role within it; it is assumed that, since schools differ and principals differ, your answers will differ. You should also keep in mind that this questionnaire is based on the assumption that all schools have latent or manifest problems that can be described in terms of group concerns, intergroup conflicts, and intragroup conflicts. The most important questions you must ask yourself as a principal are whether you are aware of the latent problems, how well you understand the manifest problems, whether you are satisfied that the problem-solving structures (committees, councils, and so forth) within your school are adequate to the task of dealing with group conflict problems, and whether you are satisfied that you have found effective role options for yourself in handling problems that stem from group pressures for change. Try to avoid minimizing the seriousness of your problems in order to present your school in a good light, and try to avoid manufacturing problems to show how aware you are. Do the best job you can of giving a realistic appraisal of your situation. After each section of the questionnaire there will be questions which can form the basis for group discussion or personal reflection. Answers to these need not be written.

I. School composition

Fill in the following chart (Figure 2-1) with approximate percentages indicating the proportion of each racial, religious, and ethnic group in your school.

Fill in the next chart (Figure 2-2) with approximate percentages indicating the proportion of socioeconomic groups within each racial, religious, and ethnic group. This chart refers to families whose children attend your school.

Group discussion or self-awareness questions

1. In what areas did you have difficulty estimating the composition of your school? Why?
2. Do you feel it is important for a principal to be aware of the groups listed above or should he try as much as possible not to think in terms of group differences?
3. How realistic are you about group differences? Do you tend to deny their importance in order to guard against being seen as prejudiced (e.g., "I treat people as people and do not even notice if they are black or white.")? Do you tend, on the other hand, to stereotype groups by assuming all members think and act alike and therefore any member speaks for his group? Can you differentiate valid generalizations about groups (those that hold for 70 percent of the group with 30 percent exceptions) from stereotypes (those that have a 30 percent kernel of truth but are untrue 70 percent of the time)?

II. Change concerns

Looking back at the charts of school composition, circle those boxes indicating groups which have actively sought (or are currently seeking) significant changes in school (e.g., changes in disciplinary policy, curriculum, school-community relations, participation in decision making, and so forth) or groups which have actively exerted pressure against proposed changes.

Now list the changes sought or opposed by the groups you have identified. If, for example, you can identify change pressures as coming primarily from a specific socioeconomic level within a given racial or religioethnic

RACE

GROUP	Black	White	American Indian	Oriental
Parents				
Teachers				
Students				

RELIGION

GROUP	Protestant	Catholic	Jewish
Parents			
Teachers			
Students			

ETHNIC ORIGIN
(ancestral nationalities)

GROUP	Italian	Irish	English	Polish	German	Puerto Rican	Cuban	Chinese	West Indian	African	Japanese	Chicano	Slavic	Other (specify)
Parents														
Teachers														
Students														

FIGURE 2-1. Chart used to determine racial, religious, and ethnic composition of a school

LEVEL	RACE				RELIGION		
	Black	White	American Indian	Oriental	Protestant	Catholic	Jewish
Upper socioeconomic							
Middle socioeconomic							
Lower socioeconomic							

LEVEL	ETHNIC ORIGIN (ancestral nationalities)													
	Italian	Irish	English	Polish	German	Puerto Rican	Cuban	Chinese	West Indian	African	Japanese	Chicano	Slavic	Other (specify)
Upper socioeconomic														
Middle socioeconomic														
Lower socioeconomic														

FIGURE 2-2. Chart used to determine relation between socioeconomic level and racial, religious, and ethnic background

group, please do so. If, on the other hand, you see certain changes or opposition to change as stemming from black students regardless of social class, from parents regardless of race, and so forth, indicate exactly what general group you are referring to. Concentrate on the three or four groupings whose change concerns have had the greatest impact or have posed the greatest problems for the school.

Looking again at the chart, what change concerns would you anticipate as likely to arise in the near future? List new concerns you would anticipate from groups which have been active and latent concerns which you think may surface from groups which have not yet actively exercised pressure for or against change.

Group discussion or self-awareness questions

1. What change concerns that have arisen in recent years took you by surprise?
2. Describe an instance in which you were aware of a change concern but had difficulty understanding why those involved felt as they did.
3. Describe a situation in which you feel you understood the problem but had difficulty finding or executing an intervention to solve the problem.

III. Mechanisms

What mechanisms exist for individuals or groups who wish to propose changes? For example, what structures (student government, faculty committees, parent organizations, advisory groups, others) are set up as vehicles for consideration of change problems within your school and what procedures are established for recommendation of changes to these bodies, to the principal, or to other authoritative sources within the school system?

Which of these mechanisms have been used recently, and how effectively have they operated? (Give an example for each.)

Describe any instances in which groups have attempted to press change concerns through strategies other than the utilization of existing mechanisms (for example, demonstrations, written demands).

What new mechanisms, if any, can you identify which might be needed to handle change problems which have either not been successfully handled by existing mechanisms or have up to now been approached through the other strategies described in the previous question?

Group discussion or self-awareness questions

1. Do existing mechanisms for change tend to involve a representative sample of groups within your school, or do they tend to be utilized only by some portions of your school constituencies?
2. If you do not have full participation, what speculations do you have as to the reasons for persons not participating? Are your student, parent, and teacher groups looked upon as "company unions"?
3. What racial, socioeconomic or religioethnic parent groups can you identify which can generally be described as feeling: a) uncomfortable or shy about participation in school affairs; b) generally at ease in dealing with

school personnel; c) very much at ease in dealing with school personnel, even to the point of feeling they know better how to run the schools than school people do?

4. In what circumstances is student, parent, teacher or community participation in decision making necessary if change decisions are to be agreed upon, understood, and implemented? What kinds of decisions about change do not require involvement of other constituencies in addition to administration?

IV. Principal's roles (See "Role Options for the Principal" within the chapter)

The following chart (Figure 2-3) contains a list of ten roles which a principal may play in change situations. Indicate, by checking the appropriate box, which roles you have used, how frequently you have used the roles, how comfortable you feel in playing each role, and how effective you have found each role in handling change problems.

ROLES	Frequently	Occasionally	Seldom	Never	Very comfortable	Moderately comfortable	Mildly uncomfortable	Very uncomfortable	Very effective	Moderately effective	Somewhat ineffective	Very ineffective
Initiator												
Stimulator												
Reactor												
Implementor												
Conduit												
Orchestrator-Mediator												
Persuader-Dissuader												
Advocate												
Ombudsman												
Nonactor												

FIGURE 2-3. Roles of the principal in change situations

Group discussion or self-awareness questions

1. In dealing with changes which stir conflicts among racial, socioeconomic or religio-ethnic groups, what have you found to be a) the advantages of the roles described, b) the pitfalls of the roles described?
2. What roles have you used which are not included in the list?
3. Do you tend to have a consistent "style," usually playing a very similar role, or do you find that your role varies considerably?
4. What criteria do you use to decide when to intervene actively, when to play a low-key role or stay out of the situation, and when to play a "third-party" or middle-man role?

V. Principal intervention in group conflict situations

As you consider the groups which compose your school, the change concerns of each group, the existing and improvised mechanisms for change which have been utilized and the role you have played in dealing with change problems, you may want to pay special attention to those issues which involve a real or perceived conflict of group interests and therefore tend to lead to polarization among groups in the school. These tend to be the most difficult situations for the principal to deal with, and they also tend to have the greatest destructive potential toward the climate of school life. In reviewing your answers to previous questions, choose three change situations involving explicit or implicit group conflict over proposed change in the school (curriculum, discipline, other) in which you intervened:

1. A situation in which you intervened successfully.
2. A situation in which your intervention had little effect.
3. A situation in which the problem worsened, despite your intervention.

Describe each situation, indicating the nature of the problem and the groups involved, the way in which the problem came to your attention, your intervention (what you did and why), the effect of your intervention, and your opinion as to why your intervention met with the described results.

Group discussion or self-awareness questions

1. Did you feel you were able to communicate with all significant groups involved or were there some who misunderstood you, heard you correctly, but disregarded what you said or would not listen to you? If so, why do you feel this occurred?
2. How do you feel you were viewed by the various faculty, parent, student and community groups in each of the situations described: as a change advocate, as a neutral party, as an advocate of maintaining the status quo?
3. Did you have any difficulty keeping your personal opinions and feelings separate from your professional role? Do you think that others misinterpreted your motives?

VI. Summary and evaluation

The sequence of this instrument is designed to enable a principal to develop a profile of the composition of his school, the change concerns of groups involved in school life, the structural mechanisms through which change can be considered, and his own role in dealing with problems of change, particularly in group conflict situations. Change situations may cause problems for a principal in a variety of ways, some of which are suggested by the questions included in the instrument. Some of these may be beyond his control, but his own role is one aspect of the situation which he can do something about. This is the reason for asking the principal to examine his own awareness, understanding, options for intervention, and so forth. If he is unaware of any group concerns, either obvious or latent, he may be unprepared when problems arise. If he is aware of a concern but does not know the "why" behind group desires for change, he may be liable to misinterpret situations. If there are not adequate standard operative mechanisms to deal with change problems in the school, he may find himself embroiled in disruptive controversy and hurriedly improvising procedures for problem solution. Similarly, since the demands upon him to play a key role in new and difficult situations are increasing, it is important that he examine closely his own interventions and be clearly conscious of the strategic decisions which underlie the postures he adopts regarding change. There is little hope that any single posture, strategy, role, or technique can be relied upon to work in all situations. Often postures which are effective in one situation may not be in another; a principal with one style of administration is thus unlikely to be as effective as one who has a variety of options on tap. Many of the traditional approaches to the exercise of authority which are second nature to many principals and have worked well in the past and still work well in many situations are meeting with increasing challenge from students, parents, teachers, and community groups in situations where group conflicts are involved. The major intent of this instrument is to provide a systematic means for the principal to examine the state of his school and the repertoire of roles and structural mechanisms available to him for dealing with change problems. The instrument is designed to enable a principal to step back from the situation in his school and examine it as systematically and objectively as possible.

In light of these goals, please respond to the following evaluation questions regarding the instrument:
1. What have you found most helpful about this instrument?
2. What have you found least helpful?
3. How would you change it, add to it, or delete from it in order to make it a more effective learning experience for principals?

NOTES

1. Depending upon the composition of a given school system, paraprofessional and nonprofessional employees of the system may also constitute important groups exerting pressure for change.

2. The model referred to was developed by the Boston University Human Relations Laboratory.

3. R. R. Blake and Jane S. Mouton, *The Managerial Grid* (Houston, Tex.: Gulf Publishing Company, 1964), exemplifies this format.

4. The In-Basket exercise, described in J. W. Pfeiffer and J. E. Jones, *A Handbook of Structural Experiences for Human Relations Training*, Vol. II (Iowa City, Iowa: University Associates Press, 1970), is an example of this model.

5. See Appendix D for an illustrative questionnaire.

6. James F. Small and Max Birnbaum, "The Structured Group Interview," *Training and Development Journal* (September 1971).

7. The introduction and preliminary discussion preceding the sample questionnaire in Appendix D is designed to serve this purpose.

8. See Kenneth D. Benne and Max Birnbaum, "Change Does Not Have to Be Haphazard," *School Review*, 68 (No. 3, 1960).

THREE

PREPARING THE ORGANIZATION FOR EFFECTIVE RESPONSE

Alan K. Gaynor

When I see I am doing it wrong there is a part of me that wants to keep on doing it the same way anyway and even starts looking for reasons to justify the continuation.

Hugh Prather[1]

One of the problems in saying you want to help anyone is the awful presumption implicit in the very statement. Or, as somebody once said, "We resist the temptation to take advice a lot better than most of us are able to resist the temptation to give it." With these caveats firmly in place, this chapter is, nevertheless, addressed to that part of each of us which *is* willing to concede that there may be some better ways if only somebody could help us to find out what they are.

Three diagnostic frameworks may be helpful in thinking more systematically about the principalship and ways of behaving effectively as an educational leader in a school building. The first of these relates to a diagnostic approach called role analysis. Role analysis has to do with what the principal does and what people think he ought to do. The important people, the significant others who have various expectations of the principal, define what is called the role set. These people or, more accurately, sets of people, include teachers, students, parents, citizens, higher administrators, and school board members, among others. Generally there is variation among role expectations, variation that can sometimes be intense and that can cause considerable psychological or political discomfort for the principal.[2] Such role conflict can be analyzed, and strategies that may lead to improved leader effectiveness can be developed for dealing with it.

Somewhat related to role analysis but focusing more upon expectations for specific outputs (programs, policies, regulations, and allocations of funds and personnel) than upon tasks is a second framework for diagnosis based on political analysis.[3] This chapter suggests some questions concerned persons might want to ask about various groups and important individuals in the community power structure.

The third framework is more eclectic and deals with the general rubric of administrative behavior. It involves important action variables and subvariables, including goal setting and planning, organization development, decision making, and administrative style, among others.

This chapter also describes diagnostic tools that may be helpful in using these frameworks to diagnose principal performance. Although these instruments are exploratory in nature, they have been designed to help in thinking about the principalship and about alternative ways to operate in the role.

ROLE ANALYSIS

One of the frameworks has to do with defining the role of the principal, separate from describing the person of the principal. The role is defined by a set of expectations, including those which the principal has for himself and those which are held for him by significant others.

Expectations are, of course, statements about the way things ought to be, rather than the way things are. Related to expectations are perceptions about actual behavior, both the principal's perceptions of his own behavior and others' perceptions of his behavior. Questions in the principalship role subdomain include:

1. What expectations does the principal hold for himself? What are his major goals and priorities? What is his vision of the future for the

school: One year from now? Three years from now? Five years from now? Ten years from now?

2. Are the principal's expectations of himself consistent with those others hold for him?

3. Are the principal's perceptions of the expectations of others accurate?

4. Are the principal's perceptions of his own behavior consistent with the perceptions of others?

5. Do others perceive his view of the principalship as consistent with theirs?

6. Is the principal's behavior consistent with his expectations for himself?

7. Is the principal's behavior consistent with the expectations others hold for him?

8. Does the principal perceive his own behavior as consistent with the expectations others hold for him?

To recapitulate, performance criteria related to role analysis and role behavior would include the following:

1. The effective principal knows himself and articulates clearly what he hopes to achieve in both the short and the long term.

2. The effective principal knows significant others around him and articulates accurately how their expectations, goals, and priorities, both as individuals and as groups, compare with his own.

3. The effective principal knows, and can describe accurately, how significant others see him.

4. The effective principal behaves in a way that is (a) consistent with the expectations, goals, and priorities of significant others, or (b) calculated to alter, with some reasonable probability of success, the expectations, goals, and priorities of significant others in directions consistent with his own.

POLITICAL ANALYSIS

Other criteria are defined for the principal within a political context, a context that includes elements both within the school and beyond it. As the old saying goes, "You gotta know the territory." This sage advice has become increasingly relevant for the school principal in recent years, especially in urban districts where ideologically diverse constituencies have become increasingly vocal and more active politically.

The political field surrounding and transcending the school is comprised of groups, both formal and informal, and influential individuals. This field is a complex and shifting one, often seeming to change both over time and with respect to specific issues. At any given time, there are active elements and passive, latent elements. In an instant passive elements can become active, and some of the most intensely active elements can appear quiet and disinterested. For the confused principal, discerning the forest for the political trees may appear to be an impossible task.

If there is any order in this apparent disarray, it would seem to be related to the distribution of values (ideologies) present in the community. Although every community has an identifiable number of key people (general elites), most studies of political power structures suggest that patterns of influence in decision making vary from issue to issue. These findings, however, do vary from one community to another.[4] Apparently the question of why and how issues motivate activism among groups is related to the underlying distribution of values in the community and the ways in which specific issues tap concerns generated by these values. One measure of the effectiveness of the principal may be the extent to which he is explicitly aware of the various political elements in his school community and the issues that are likely to motivate their active participation in the political life of the school.

Within this context, the effective principal must be cognizant not only of strong signals emanating from the political environment, but also of weak signals. Indicative of this awareness is an ability, uncanny to some, to foresee the future (at least to the extent of explicit probability statements) and to develop proactive programs and strategies responsive to this future.[5] The effective principal is more often able to view events in the political environment objectively. He is able to distinguish accurately those actions directed against him as principal from those directed against him as a person. As a result, he is less likely to behave defensively and more likely to be open to suggestions for alternative modes of action. The ineffective principal, on the other hand, is less likely to display future vision and more likely to display a kind of administrative tunnel vision. He is less aware of weak signals and less adaptive in his patterns of administrative response. He is more likely to view events in the political environment subjectively, as being directed more at the person than at the principal, and, therefore, also more likely to respond reactively in an environment of constant and recurring crises.

In a political analysis, the following questions might be asked:

1. Which major groups in the school and community have expressed concern at one time or another about the school, its policies, and its programs?

2. Who are the present and potential leaders of these groups?

3. What are the major values held by each group? To what kinds of issues does each typically attend? How have these changed over time?

4. Which groups seem most stable: Organizationally? Ideologically?

5. What kinds of political resources are available to each group?

6. What political strategies does each group typically employ? How have these changed over time?

7. On balance, do educational politics in the school community seem to be:

  (a) dominated by a single political-ideological faction?
  (b) dominated by two or three major competing factions?
  (c) active, but competitive among many groups?
  (d) of little concern to citizens in the community but dominated
      primarily by the superintendent and the professional staff?[6]

8. Who, if any, are the highly influential individuals in the school and community? What are their values and salient concerns? What are their bases of power?

9. Who, if any, are the latent individuals and groups, those who have not yet exercised political power on the school, but who might do so in the future? What issues are likely to arouse them and how are they likely to act once aroused? What political resources are available to them?

10. Do demands, both active and latent, tend toward declarations of concern, position statements, or other symbolic actions, toward new policies and regulations, toward new programs requiring significant reallocations of physical resources, or toward opportunities for certain groups to participate more in making decisions for the

school? What patterns of escalation and reaction, if any, are evident in the changing nature of demands over time?

11. To what extent are significant demands and political actions directed toward the principal as a person? To what extent are they primarily directed toward him as an official representative of the school system?

In other words, performance criteria related to the politics of effective principalship include:

1. a knowledge of the key people, how they are organized, what turns them on (and off), how they are likely to react in specific situations, and what they can do for the school (or against it);

2. a sense of what the future will, can, and should look like—in the community, in the wider social and educational world, and, therefore, in the school (or whatever the school is to become in the world of the future);

3. an ability to work with widely diverse groups of people in the school and community, to provide channels through which demands can be articulated, and to provide structures and processes for aggregating conflicting demands. This can be accomplished by identifying and building upon areas of common agreement, by using sophisticated group processes where appropriate to minimize feelings of territoriality and hostility,[7] and by adjusting policy to accommodate unbridgeable value differences among such diverse constituencies as racial and ethnic groups, social class groups, or individuals.[8]

ANALYSIS OF ADMINISTRATIVE BEHAVIOR

Any analysis of administrative behavior is concerned, first of all, with the ways in which administrative actions can usefully be classified. Administrative behavior is not simply a matter of responding to problems. It should be viewed more broadly, in terms of preparing the school organization for responsive action. With this frame of reference the principal is seen not as the decision maker, for the organization makes the decisions. Rather, he is seen as the person with primary responsibility for the development of the school as an adaptive organization. Given this definition of the role of principal, a number of important functions suggest themselves as criteria for diagnosing performance.

Preparing a Sense of the Future

One of the key functions of the principal was discussed in connection with political analysis. It has to do with preparing a sense of the future. Activities in support of this function include:

Broad-scan information seeking. Consistent with building and maintaining a sensitivity to weak signals in the school environment, an effective principal develops the most powerful antennae tuned to the broadest range of information sources. Data retrieved from the environment in this way become the basis for inductive problem definition, which is essential to building proactive response systems.[9]

Personal value awareness. Building a vision of the future is really a dynamic transition between the reality as given and one's own personal value commitment. The effective principal needs to know who he is, both philosophically and ideologically. He needs to communicate who he is to other people and to understand who they are in relation to his own value commitments. Surely this ability is an important element of charisma, a quality which constitutes a significant part of leadership as opposed to mere management.

Personal goal setting. Having thought about where he thinks the school might want to be one, five, or ten years from now and having considered this vision of the future in the light of his own personal value commitments, the effective principal engages in a systematic process of personal goal identification. These cannot be final goals since the determination of final goals is an organizational, not a personal, process. The principal must, however, make explicit his own ideas about where to go and how to get there.

Personal planning. Having developed a set of personal goals to guide him in the future, the effective principal then outlines, at least in broad strokes, the organization he will need to move the school into the kind of future he envisions. He begins to develop a set of very flexible, very tentative organizational blueprints to provide a useful starting point for future-oriented activity.

Organizational Development

A second key function of the effective principal is that of organizational development. Activities supporting this function include:

Building organizational trust. It has already been suggested that broad-scan information seeking represents a significant activity of the effective principal. While it is significant, information seeking is not, in itself, sufficient. The information obtained must also be valid, which requires an atmosphere of trust. Students of organizational development have shown that, where trust is lacking, subordinates only provide superiors with information carefully selected to protect themselves and their interests. One important measure of organizational trust is, therefore, the completeness and reliability of the information which the principal is able to acquire.

Building organizational mechanisms. It follows from the position taken earlier (that the principal is the person with major responsibility for the development of the school as an adaptive organization) that the kinds of structures which the principal is able to initiate constitute another measure of his leadership effectiveness. One kind of structure which the effective principal needs is an efficient management information system. This includes an information-gathering subsystem with major components devoted to political awareness and institutional research. It also includes a data-processing subsystem for data storage, retrieval, and analysis. This terminology is not intended to suggest the need for sophisticated computer technology. That could be a potentially useful approach to the problem, but experience with computer-based management information systems has shown the danger of information overload as opposed to data scarcity. The development of management information should be geared as closely as possible to the demonstrated needs of decision making and inductive problem definition.

A second kind of structure needed is an adaptive human infrastructure. This is composed of groups of teachers, students, parents, and other members of the school community systematically involved in identifying problem signals, defining problems (present and future), identifying potential resources and constraints, and developing alternative strategies. These groups are engaged in policy making that is responsive to a sense of the future.

A third kind of structure involves building and maintaining relationships. This requires attention to clarifying roles in the human infrastructure. In a sense it is concerned with refining an ever-changing role structure.

Responding to Immediate Demands

A third key function of the effective principal is that of responding to immediate demands. Activities that support this function include:

Priority setting. One of the great difficulties an administrator faces, especially a less effective administrator, is assigning priority decisions. Both time and tempo are important factors in responding to immediate demands. Some things need to be done immediately; some can or should be postponed; others should be ignored until some as yet unforeseen moment. Priority setting is an important measure of administrative effectiveness.

Preparing for decisions. Since "the best laid plans of mice and men gang aft agley," even the most farsighted principal is faced with immediate decisions. In short- as well as long-term decision making, criteria of effectiveness include quality of information seeking, appropriateness of delegation, and appropriateness of interpersonal and intergroup involvement. One can seek out too much information, especially given the constraints of time, or one can seek out too little. With respect to delegation and involvement, principals often involve others intensively at precisely the wrong times. Less effective principals tend to involve others in routine matters that the administrator should handle, and they fail to involve others in vital, professional policy decisions.

Means of communication. An important, but often neglected aspect of administrative behavior, especially in responding to immediate demands, is the administrator's ability to communicate. Less effective administrators may be less aware of the psychological effect that nonverbal communication has upon people. They may be less aware of important meanings often associated with territoriality and means of communication. Whether the principal asks another person to come to his office, meets him on his own ground, or meets him in a neutral place such as a local restaurant may be important. It may also make a difference whether or not the principal sits behind his desk while talking with that person, writes him a letter, or calls him on the telephone. As McLuhan pointed out, "The medium is the message," and certain styles of communication, especially those that are heavily impersonal, tend to communicate "bureaucracy." Other styles may indicate concern and consideration. Sensitivity to such nuances may be a measure of administrative effectiveness.

Administrative Style

Administrative style is a global concept that seeks to characterize a whole range of administrative behaviors. Those who have studied leader behavior and have dealt with the idea of administrative style generally emphasize two basic factors: the administrator's concern for production and his concern for people.[10]

Early research with small groups identified and compared three types of leadership style: democratic, authoritative, and laissez-faire.[11] More recent research suggests that effective leader behavior is responsive to the situation,[12] to the maturity of the group relative to the task,[13] and to a number of significant problem attributes.[14] The concept of administrative style seems more and more to be a useful but complex basis for diagnosis.

RECAPITULATION: PERFORMANCE CRITERIA IN ADMINISTRATIVE BEHAVIOR

1. The effective principal maintains effective communication with information sources covering a wide range of perspectives on the school.

2. The effective principal builds trust in widely diverse constituencies, trust which increases the validity of the information he is able to collect and the accuracy with which he can assess needs and define potential problems well in advance of crisis.

3. The effective principal builds his own future vision in a continuous exchange between his own personal values and the perspectives of others as they are communicated to him.

4. The effective principal stimulates structures through which multiple perspectives are continuously channeled, needs are assessed, and problems are defined, and through which action is continuously taken to achieve the organization's vision of the future. He builds among all constituents of the school and the community a feeling of belonging, a sense of identity in terms of goals, and a belief in the rationality of policies.

5. The effective principal works primarily to build an organization which defines and works toward long-range goals. Even in responding to immediate demands (unavoidable even in the most responsive and participative organizations), the effective principal sets priorities and prepares carefully for decisions.[15] He identifies items that need to be dealt with immediately, later, or not at all; he gathers sufficient information to define each problem and, subsequently, to define and evaluate the most promising alternative actions and potential, unin-

tended consequences within the limits of time and priority; he involves others in the decision-making processes in ways consistent with their expectations and desires and in accord with their interests and expertise; and he employs means of communication based on sensitivity to nonverbal meanings as well as on considerations of efficiency and bureaucratic control.

SOME MEASURES OF PERFORMANCE

The first part of this chapter provides a conceptual framework within which to think about the principalship. This framework, consisting of three fairly broad diagnostic subframeworks, can serve as a basis for reflection on, and evaluation and diagnosis of, the problems faced by principals. It can also serve as a guide for pre- and in-service education of principals.

The approaches to measurement contained in this part of the chapter are intended to aid those concerned with effective principal performance. The instruments proposed represent another effort to specify leadership competencies for principals, and, although these competencies are somewhat impressionistic at times, they are observable and measurable.

Two of these instruments—the Action Analysis Profile and the Means of Communication Profile—have been tested with persons playing the role of the principal in simulated school environments.[16] Two others—the Task Analysis Profile and the Administrative Style Analysis Profile—are being tested with practicing principals, teachers, and citizens in actual school situations. All of these efforts have been formative in nature, intended to refine the instruments and develop workable procedures for administering and interpreting them. They are not final validation efforts.

Role Analysis

One diagnostic framework dealt with earlier concerned the role of the principal. Suggested criteria of effectiveness included the degree of correspondence between the principal's self-expectations and those of significant others for him and the accuracy of the principal's perceptions of the expectations of significant others. It was intimated that wide discrepancies in the first or marked inaccuracies in the second might indicate potential or present areas of difficulty in an existing situation, the assumption being that effective leadership does not exist in a vacuum but in a real situation.

The prototype instruments developed here can serve as possible models for describing and comparing the expectations of the principal and significant others in his role set. Each can be used with persons in different role positions: principal, teacher, superintendent, parent, interested citizen, and so forth. The principal, himself, can use the instruments to describe either his self-expectations or the expectations that he feels others hold for him. Various comparisons and contrasts can then be drawn.

TASK ANALYSIS PROFILE (TAP)

Directions

A number of tasks are listed below, each of which has been identified by teachers, principals, and superintendents as one associated with the role of the school principal. However, not everyone agrees about the priority of each of these tasks for the principal, nor about the specific role the principal should play in accomplishing each task.

For each of the tasks listed, you should indicate (a) the priority you assign to the task as being for the *principal* and (b) the specific role *you think the principal should play* in accomplishing the task.

Priorities

Priorities are assigned on a scale of 0-10. For each task listed, place a zero in the column headed "Task priority" on the TAP Scoring Sheet (Figure 3-1) if you think that the task is not the job of the principal at all. Place a 10 in the column only if you think the task is a critical part of the principal's job. Use the numbers 1-9 to indicate priorities from low to high. Assigning a 5 to a task would indicate that it is of moderate priority for the principal.

Role of the Principal in Accomplishing the Task

The principal may have one or more roles to play in accomplishing any particular task (or he may be seen as having no role at all with respect to that task). Indicate on the scoring sheet the role or roles you think the principal should play in accomplishing each task by dividing a total of 10 points among the several roles the principal may play in accomplishing each task.

If you think that any one of the roles is precisely the one the principal should play, and no other, you should assign all 10 points to that role. If you think that a particular task is not one in which the principal should be involved at all, assign all 10 points to "No Role."

If you think that the principal should be involved in accomplishing the task in several different roles, you should give points to each of the several roles you think he should play. However, you may want to give more points to one role

ROLE OF THE PRINCIPAL[a]

TASK NUMBER	No role	Doer	Director	Delegator	Coor-dinator	Facil-itator	Moti-vator	Participant	Evaluator	TASK PRIORITY[b]
1										
2										
3										
4										
5										
6										
7										
8										
9										
10										
etc.										

[a]For each task, distribute a total of ten (10) points across one or more roles.
[b]Mark each task with a priority rating (0-10 points each).

FIGURE 3-1. Task analysis profile scoring sheet

than another (because you think it is a more important role for the principal to play), although points may be assigned equally to several different roles. *Just be sure that for each task the total number of points you assign is equal to 10.* Use the TAP Scoring Sheet to record your responses. Use the back of the scoring sheet to write any comments you may have about the task items or to write any additional items which you think should be included.

Definition of Roles on the TAP Scoring Sheet

No role: The task may or may not be an important one for *somebody* to do, but it is not a task for the principal to be involved in.

Doer: The task should be done by the principal, himself.

Director: The principal not only should delegate the task, but he should supervise its accomplishment closely and directly.

Delegator: The principal should delegate the task, but need not be involved in direct and close supervision of its accomplishment.

Coordinator: The task should be done by others, but the principal should play an integrative role.

Facilitator: The task should be done by others, but the principal should be available to provide whatever support he can.

Motivator: The principal should stimulate others to accomplish the task.

Participant: The principal should be involved with others as a colleague (peer relationship) in accomplishing the task.

Evaluator: The task should be done by others, but the principal should be involved in judging its outcomes.

Tasks

1. Collecting, preparing, and disseminating information within the school and the school system
2. Evaluating student performance
3. Implementing educational innovations
4. Assessing educational needs
5. Improving staff interaction
6. Recruiting professional personnel for the school
7. Working with other educational agencies in the community (e.g., private and parochial schools)
8. Working with noneducational public agencies in the community (e.g., police, fire, health, youth, welfare, and judicial agencies)
9. Managing school budgeting and accounting
10. Maintaining the status of the school in the community
11. Planning the instructional program
12. Maintaining the status of the school in the school system
13. Selecting and hiring professional personnel for the school
14. Communicating performance information to individual staff members
15. Seeing to his own professional growth
16. Developing educational goals
17. Evaluating teacher aides and other similar subprofessional staff performance

18. Interpreting and using measures of school operation effectiveness
19. Orienting new staff members
20. Dismissing professional personnel from the school
21. Providing information in the form of reports to superiors
22. Evaluating professional staff performancè
23. Transferring professional personnel from the school
24. Enforcing school procedures, rules, and regulations
25. Developing and maintaining contacts with formal and informal groups in the local community
26. Seeing to the professional growth of the clerical and custodial staff
27. Seeing to the professional growth of teacher aides and other similar subprofessional staff
28. Identification and resolution of long-range problems contributing to immediate pressures on the school
29. Promoting and granting tenure to professional personnel in the school
30. Developing performance criteria for teachers and other professional personnel, including assistant principals
31. Assessing the educational needs, desires, and attitudes of the local community
32. Evaluating educational innovations
33. Implementing educational goals in the school
34. Seeking additional materials, funds, or personnel for the school from the central administration and the board of education
35. Handling staff grievances
36. Articulating and communicating educational goals to the local community
37. Maintaining routine student discipline
38. Determining school procedures, rules, and regulations
39. Articulating and communicating educational goals to teachers and students
40. Responding to local community disorders
41. Scheduling classes
42. Developing performance criteria for students
43. Hiring, firing, and promoting clerical and custodial personnel in the school
44. Hiring, firing, and promoting teacher aides and other similar subprofessional personnel in the school
45. Seeing to the professional growth of the professional staff
46. Allocating instructional resources among teachers and other school personnel (e.g., supplies, equipment, instructional materials, physical space)
47. Dealing with major school disturbances
48. Seeking additional funds, materials, or personnel for the school from persons or organizations outside of the school system
49. Developing and maintaining contacts with parents and other individuals in the local community
50. Developing criteria for evaluating his own performance as principal
51. Formulating within the school procedures to measure the effectiveness of the school's operation
52. Evaluating clerical and custodial staff performance

53. Your task (Please specify.): _____

_____

_____

54. Your task (Please specify.): _____

_____

_____

55. Your task (Please specify.): _____

_____

Add any more tasks you think it is important for the school principal to perform. Add as many as you wish. (Use additional sheets as necessary.)

Administrative Style. Whereas the Task Analysis Profile is designed to assist the respondent in describing his perception of the functional content of the principal's role, the Administrative Style Analysis Profile is designed to help him describe his perceptions about the process of the principal's role. Essentially, it provides a format within which he can rate his feelings about different ways in which principals can behave. Like the Task Analysis Profile, it can be used to record the perceptions not only of the principal but also of others.

ADMINISTRATIVE STYLE ANALYSIS PROFILE (ASAP)

Directions

Each of the following statements describes a way in which a school principal ought to behave. Most people will agree with some of the statements and disagree with others. Also, they will usually agree or disagree with some more strongly than others. Each statement describes an opinion which some people hold, whereas others do not. Obviously, there are no right or wrong answers.

In the space provided on the ASAP Scoring Sheet (Figure 3-2), write a number from -2 to +2 for each of the twenty statements. Use the back of the ASAP Scoring Sheet to write any comments you may have about the statements and to write additional statements you think should be included.

Use the following scoring guide in marking your responses:

Strongly agree	+ 2
Agree	+ 1
Uncertain	0
Disagree	- 1
Strongly disagree	- 2

You should respond in some way to each of the twenty items. Any item to which you do not respond will be scored as "Uncertain."

Statements

1. If the principal is really an effective administrator, his staff should be able to run the school largely without him.

Statement number	Scoring response	Statement number	Scoring response
1		13	
2		14	
3		15	
4		16	
5		17	
6		18	
7		19	
8		20	
9		21	
10		22	
11		23	
12		24	

FIGURE 3-2. Administrative style analysis profile scoring sheet

2. The effective principal must be aware of national trends and movements and should not be too easily swayed by peculiarly local demands.
3. As a school principal, it is best to communicate as often as possible in writing. It is efficient and leaves no doubt as to what was really said.
4. The primary work of a school principal is right in his own school. If people want to see him, they should be able to find him in his office.
5. As a school principal, it is much easier to deal effectively with people if you get out of your office and meet them as often as possible right where *they* live or work.
6. The principal is the major voice of the professional staff in the administrative hierarchy and should do all he can to reflect his teachers' views in matters of policy making.
7. Nobody wants to hurt people's feelings, but the effective principal may often have to do that in order to see that his school does the job it is expected to do.

8. The school principal should deal largely with groups, formal and informal, in making decisions and in developing policy.

9. As a school principal, it is the personal touch which, more often than not, makes the difference between the effective and ineffective principal.

10. The school principal should spend a lot of time talking with individuals—teachers, students, parents, and others who relate to the school.

11. As a school principal, it's good to get out to talk with people, but there's so much work to be done that, in terms of efficiency, it is really better to have them come to your office to talk.

12. The principal should consult others prior to making decisions, but he alone is primarily responsible for making the final decisions.

13. As a school principal, talking with people face to face (or by telephone if you cannot meet) is almost always the best way of communicating.

14. The principal, more than anyone else on the school staff, really represents the kids.

15. The principal as administrator is, more than anybody, a "man in the middle" trying to balance the needs and values of students, teachers, administration, and community.

16. Generally, the way to make the best decisions is to involve groups of people in making them.

17. The principal is the superintendent's representative in the building and is primarily responsible to the superintendent.

18. The principal, if he is to be truly effective, must reflect the attitudes and desires of the local community as accurately as possible in his administration.

19. Policies and regulations can be changed, but, until they are, the school principal should see that they are carried out.

20. The building principal should be essentially "an educational radical," working with students, innovative teachers, and people in the local community to make fundamental changes in the educational structure.

21. The principal should be involved not only in managing the school but, if necessary to achieve his goals and those of the school as an organization, he should also involve himself in a wide range of political activities in the local and school-system community.

22. The principal, as much as anyone in the school, should represent the tone of the neighborhood.

23. Having clarified his own goals and values, the principal should maneuver, politically if necessary, to translate them into effective policy. In the best sense of the word, he should become an "educational lobbyist."

24. The principal should be aware of and utilize not only his own expertise and that of his staff but also that of lay and professional people outside of the school.

It is anticipated that both the Task Analysis Profile and the Administrative Style Analysis Profile will prove useful as diagnostic tools in terms of the opportunities they offer not only for developing comparative data about differing perceptions within the principal's role set but also for identifying possible inconsistencies and imbalances in the perceptions and behaviors of the principal, himself.

Principals may discover that their expectations and behaviors are not consistent with those others hold for them. Alternatively, principals may find that their behavior is inconsistent with their own stated priorities and expectations. Principals may also find that their stated priorities are inconsistent with limitations of time and psychic energy.

Such insight may provide bases for significant modification of behavior to achieve greater consistency with regard to realities of time and personal capacity, one's own priorities and expectations, and the priorities and expectations of significant others. Possibilities for growth on the part of the principal seem most likely, of course, if discrepancies can be noted under conditions that are fundamentally supportive and not personally judgmental. In this context, the central office supervisory task is a critical one.

Political Analysis

The approach taken here is a marked contrast to that taken in the previous section. In seeking to help the principal to look at the perceptions he and others have of his role, we relied fairly heavily upon two structured instruments. Of course it will be evident to the reader that, even where structured instrumentation is used to support a laboratory method of supervision in which data are generated by and fed back to the client, a whole fabric of dialogue and interpersonal transaction envelops the use of the instruments and alters their effectiveness. In this section and the next, therefore, structured instruments will not be used. Rather, the approach is clinical, leaning more toward structured interviews, logkeeping, and behavior analysis with generation of feedback through the development and evaluation of action strategies implemented over time.

The Initial Interview. The political diagnostic process begins for the principal with his first formal interview with the diagnostic team,[17] when he is asked to describe either orally or in writing his perceptions of the political environment and the school in relation to that environment. This initial structured interview is designed to provide base line data against which to assess the accuracy of the principal's political awareness. Together with data from other sources, it also provides a foundation for future planning. The following suggests the kinds of information a principal might initially be asked to provide.

STRUCTURED INTERVIEW FORMAT

I. Describe the political demand and support structures of the school attendance area.
    A. Identify significant individuals, groups, and subgroups
    B. Specify for each of them the issues they relate to and the kinds of demands they are pressing upon the school
        1. Demands for program, space, materials, personnel, among other things, to be allocated in specified ways
        2. Demands for the behavior of certain individuals or groups to be regulated in specified ways
        3. Demands for participation in the system
        4. Demands for communication and information
    C. Specify for each its importance in terms of the kinds of supports (positive and negative) it can deliver
        1. Goods and services
        2. Respect (or disrespect) for regulations
        3. Voting or political activity
        4. Respect (or disrespect) for school authorities
II. Describe how the political demand and support structures have changed over time to the present and how they are likely to change further in the future.[18]
III. Discuss explicitly the extent to which the school has (or has not) met significant demands and describe strategies for meeting present and developing discrepancies between significant demands and outputs. (Such strategies should show an awareness of both constraints and potential resources for overcoming constraints.)[19]

Follow-up Data. The accuracy of the principal's perceptions of the political environment of the school will probably be checked against data obtained from a sample of relevant sources in the school and the community. For this reason it seems important that the principal's observations, and those of others, be obtained either in writing or on tape (to be subsequently transcribed) so that clear and accurate comparisons can be made.

Analysis of Administrative Behavior

In the first part of this chapter, a number of effectiveness criteria were suggested for use in analyzing administrative behavior. These were grouped under four major functional headings: preparing a sense of the future; organizational development; responding to immediate demands; administrative style. Now we can attempt to operationalize approaches to evaluate each of these areas.

Future Planning. As in the previous section dealing with political analysis, the emphasis here is upon the principal, himself, and upon his ability to articulate a sense of the future. Once again, the structured interview is used to generate basic data for analysis, planning, and assessment. The following items suggest the kinds of information a principal might initially be asked to provide.

STRUCTURED INTERVIEW FORMAT

I. Identify and describe key events and developing trends in the environment (both immediate and distant) that may herald previously unanticipated demands upon the school.

II. Describe explicitly and in some detail your own sense of the future for this school.
   A. Your own powerful value commitments and personal goals
   B. The kinds of organizational development activities you have set or are planning to set into motion to achieve goals consistent with these powerful value commitments (Plans should include some broad time schedules for meeting intermediate goals.)
      1. Policy changes you have initiated or are planning to initiate
      2. Structures and processes you have initiated to diffuse power and to widen participation in future planning and significant policy making (especially for those principals operating under conditions of high uncertainty and rapid environmental change)[20]
      3. Management information systems you have established
         a. to monitor present and potential demands and supports
         b. to monitor and to identify present and potential points of stress in the school
      4. Mechanisms you have established or are planning to establish to focus diverse activities on common goals and to mediate conflicts deriving from differences in functions and values (integrative mechanisms)

Organizational Development and Administrative Style. Important organizational mechanisms were included as diagnostic items in the previous section. Such overlap is inevitable when dealing with systematic attributes which, by definition, are highly interactive. Fortunately, this problem is more a theoretical than a practical one. What is important in the present context is that all of the key variables be attended by the principal at some point in the diagnostic process.

Organizational development and administrative style are conjoined in this section because of the apparent availability of instruments to measure their joint effects upon leader behavior and organizational climate. It seems to us that instruments such as Hemphill's Leader Behavior Description Questionnaire (LBDQ)[21] and Halpin and Croft's Organizational Climate Description Questionnaire (OCDQ)[22] can serve admirably the kinds of diagnostic purposes this project has in mind. The only caveat is that they be treated not so much as objective descriptions of what is, but rather as measures of personal perceptions, subject to all of the individual biases that this implies. In this sense they should be used in much the same ways as the Task Analysis Profile and the Administrative Style Analysis Profile are used in role analysis.

Responding to Immediate Demands. Some of the subfunctions under the general rubric of responding to immediate demands include: priority setting, preparing for decisions, attending to groups and individuals, and means of communicating.

One of the problems, which is a significant shortcoming for many administrators, is the lack of effective priority setting. In some cases, the only priority is the presence of the item on the top of the pile, either literally or figuratively (as when someone walks into his office and will not go away). One way of looking at administrative behavior in responding to problem situations, therefore, is to examine specifically the ways in which the principal does or does not set priorities. The following checklist suggests some criteria that may serve to order priorities.

PRIORITY-SETTING ANALYSIS CHECKLIST (PSAC)

1. First come, first served.
2. Subjective evaluation of the importance of the item (more or less important items first).
3. Subjective evaluation of the time the item will take (e.g., those which can be dispensed with quickly come first).
4. Subjective evaluation of the proper timing of the items in a strategic sense (some must be done now, some later, some not at all, or at least not until some new decision point as yet unknown).
5. Some other criterion which the principal defines.

Action Analysis. The Action Analysis Profile has been developed, and tested to some extent, to help identify patterns of administrative performance in simulated environments. In the "actions" and "objects of action," which constitute its basic typology, it relates both to preparing for decisions and to attending to groups and individuals:

Actions	*Objects of action*
1. Ignored the observed event	A. Files and/or written policies and regulations
2. Considered the observed event but took no action	B. Higher authority
3. Took action without involving others in a significant way before making the decision	C. Another building principal(s)
4. Referred the matter to higher authority	D. A teacher(s) and/or a subordinate administrator(s)
5. Delegated complete authority in the matter to _____	E. A student(s)
6. Delegated partial authority in the matter (with guidelines) to _____	F. A secretary
7. Discussed or made arrangements to discuss the matter with _____	G. Someone else in the school (other than a teacher, administrator, student or secretary
8. Asked for opinion, advice, or permission from _____	H. The parent of a student involved in the observed event
9. Asked for or made arrangements to get information from _____	I. An outsider
10. Directed _____	J. The faculty
11. Informed _____	K. A faculty committee
12. Explained actions to _____	L. A faculty-citizen committee
13. Created or made plans to create _____	M. A faculty-citizen-student committee
14. Communicated as a matter of courtesy to _____	N. A faculty-student committee
	O. The community
	P. A citizen committee
	Q. A citizen-student committee
	R. The student body
	S. The student organization
	T. A student committee outside of the official student organization
	U. A new policy
	V. A new program

As an instrument it represents, essentially, a taxonomy for content analysis. The data for analysis are the various actions (letters written, phone calls made, conferences held) taken by the role player and recorded on forms provided as part of the workshop materials. The data for analyzing the principal's performance in an actual on-the-job situation would have to be obtained in a somewhat different fashion.

It is suggested that, in a live situation, data can be obtained in at least two different ways:

1. The principal can keep a log in which he records the problems that arise in the course of several days (or longer) and the actions that he takes in response to those problems. Many of the problems will be immediate in nature; some will really be perceptions that the principal has of longer-range considerations.

2. An observer (perhaps a consultant or a graduate student at a nearby university) can log the principal's actions in response to situations which he observes as he trails the principal during the course of the day. In either case, the data can be analyzed for patterns of response using the Action Analysis Profile. Such an action analysis may reveal patterns of response that are inconsistent with the desired objectives of the principal.

ACTION ANALYSIS PROFILE (AAP)

Directions

The AAP is designed to provide the principal with feedback about his or her administrative behavior. It provides a system within which an observer can classify the principal's actions in fairly general categories.[22]

The classification system used employs a 14 x 22 grid: fourteen types of action and twenty-two objects of action. The first four types of action stand alone and require no objects of action to complete them. Each of the remaining ten types of action must be combined with an appropriate object of action in order to be complete.

If, for example, in dealing with a situation the principal "took action without involving others in a significant way before making the decision," the observer would note this on the AAP Scoring Sheet simply by putting the number "3" in the first space next to the number assigned to that particular observation. However, if the principal asked for or made arrangements to get information from . . . one of the teachers, the observer would put a combination number-letter on the scoring sheet—in this case "9-D." Looking at the two columns, the reader will see that the "9" indicates that the principal *sought information* and the "D" indicates that it was *sought from teacher(s) or subordinate administrator(s)*.

In a similar manner, the observer scores on the scoring sheet all actions the principal took in response to every problem incident

	OBJECTS OF ACTION																							
ACTIONS		A	B	C	D	E	F	G	H	I	J	K	L	M	N	O	P	Q	R	S	T	U	V	TOTAL
1																								
2																								
3																								
4																								
5																								
6																								
7																								
8																								
9																								
10																								
11																								
12																								
13																								
14																								
TOTAL																								

FIGURE 3-3. Action analysis profile tally grid

observed and logged. The scoring sheet permits the observer to score up to five actions for each situation.

After the observer has completed the scoring sheet, he tallies the combinations from the scoring sheet in the appropriate cells of the AAP Tally Grid. The row totals reflect the kinds of actions the principal typically takes; the column totals show the kinds of people he typically involves in his actions; and the tallies in the cells indicate how he typically puts actions and people together.

Means of Communication. The means the principal uses to communicate with people may convey, nonverbally, at least as much as the words themselves. Some means of communication, especially those which are impersonal, may suggest "bureaucracy" and "authority." Other, more personal forms of communication may suggest "approachability" and "consideration." The Means of Communication Profile was developed as a means of providing feedback to participants in simulation workshops, and it serves the same purpose for principals on the job. Again, the data for analysis can be generated either by logging or by nonparticipant observation.

MEANS OF COMMUNICATION PROFILE (MCP)

Directions

The MCP is designed to provide the principal with feedback about the ways in which he or she communicates with people.

On the MCP Tally Grid eight means of communication are listed.[23] For each event, the observer checks in the appropriate cell(s) the means of communication used by the principal. Up to three different means of communication may be tallied for each situation. Row totals reflect the means of communication typically employed by the principal.

Final Comments

The instruments presented here have been designed as diagnostic tools. They are not additive; rather, they provide profiles or patterns of perception and behavior. There are no norms, and they are not intended to be used as rating scales. Rather, they are intended to provide the principal, and those who would assist him to grow as an administrator, with ways to understand better his strengths as well as his weaknesses and utilize strategies as an administrator that capitalize upon his strengths and expose his weaknesses as little as possible. Only he, with perhaps a little help from his friends, can, how-

MEANS OF COMMUNICATION	PROBLEM INCIDENTS																						TOTAL
	1	2	3	4	5	6	7	8	9	10	11	12	13	14	15	16	17	18	19	20	21	22	
Writing																							
Telephone																							
Face-to-face (in principal's office)																							
Face-to-face (in another's office, room, home, etc.)																							
Face-to-face (in some neutral place)																							
Public meeting or assembly																							
Mass media (radio, TV, newspapers, etc.)																							
Indirect communication ("telling someone to tell someone else")																							
TOTAL																							

FIGURE 3-4. Communication profile tally grid

ever, decide which are strengths and which are weaknesses. If data generated from such instruments as these help him to do that, they have served their purpose.

NOTES

1. Hugh Prather, *Notes to Myself: My Struggle to Become a Person* (Moab, Utah: Real People Press, 1970).

2. See, for example, Robert L. Kahn *et al.*, *Organizational Stress: Studies in Role Conflict and Ambiguity* (New York: John Wiley and Sons, 1965); Neal Gross, W. S. Mason, and A. W. McEachern, *Explorations in Role Analysis: Studies of the School Superintendency Role* (New York: John Wiley and Sons, 1958).

3. See, for example, David Easton, *A Systems Analysis of Political Life* (New York: John Wiley and Sons, 1965); Gabriel A. Almond and G. Bingham Powell, Jr., *Comparative Politics: A Developmental Approach* (Boston: Little, Brown, 1966).

4. See, for example, Floyd Hunter, *Community Power Structure* (Chapel Hill: University of North Carolina Press, 1953); Robert A. Dahl, *Who Governs? Democracy and Power in an American City* (New Haven, Conn.: Yale University Press, 1961); Nelson W. Polsby, *Community Power and Political Theory* (New Haven, Conn.: Yale University Press, 1963); Laurence Iannaccone and Frank Lutz, *Politics, Power, and Policy: The Governing of Local School Districts* (Columbus, Ohio: Charles E. Merrill, 1970).

5. See, for example, the chapter, "Breakthroughs," in Joseph P. Martino, *Technological Forecasting for Decisionmaking* (New York: American Elsevier, 1972), pp. 210-249.

6. Donald J. McCarty and Charles E. Ramsey, *The School Managers: Power and Conflict in American Public Education* (Westport, Conn.: Greenwood Press, 1971).

7. See, for example, Chapter Two; see also Max Birnbaum, "The Clarification Group," in Kenneth D. Benne, Lee Bradford, Jack Gibb, and Ronald Lippitt (eds.), *The Laboratory Method of Learning and Changing* (New York: John Wiley and Sons, in press).

8. See, for example, Mario Fantini, "Options for Students, Parents, and Teachers: Public Schools of Choice," *Phi Delta Kappan,* 52 (No. 9, May 1971). One should note the assumption here that effective leadership maximizes opportunities for choice and minimizes bureaucratic uniformity for its own sake. Effective leadership accepts the burden of organizational integration inherent in diversity in order to maximize the responsiveness of the system to social and political pluralism and to rapid and continuing changes in the educational environment. For a discussion of differentiation and integration in organizations, see Paul Lawrence and Jay W. Lorsch, *Organization and Environment* (Homewood, Ill.: Richard D. Irwin, 1969).

9. Martino, *Technological Forecasting.*

10. Thomas J. Sergiovanni and Robert J. Starratt, *Emerging Patterns of Supervision: Human Perspectives* (New York: McGraw-Hill, 1971), p. 88.

11. K. Lewin, R. Lippitt, and R. White, "Leader Behavior and Member Reaction in Three 'Social Climates,' " in Dorwin Cartwright and Alvin Zander (eds.), *Group Dynamics: Research and Theory,* 2nd ed. (Evanston, Ill.: Row, Peterson, 1960).

12. Fred E. Fiedler, *A Theory of Leadership Effectiveness* (New York: McGraw-Hill, 1967).

13. Paul Hersey and Kenneth H. Blanchard, *Management of Organizational Behavior* (Englewood Cliffs, N.J.: Prentice-Hall, 1972).

14. Victor H. Vroom and Philip W. Yetton, *Leadership and Decision-Making* (Pittsburgh: University of Pittsburgh Press, 1973).

15. For a more detailed discussion of preparing for decisions, see John Hemphill, Daniel E. Griffiths, and Norman Frederiksen, *Administrative Performance and Personality* (New York: Bureau of Publications, Teachers College, Columbia University, 1962).

16. Alan K. Gaynor, "Playing the Role of the Principal: Patterns of Administrative Response," paper presented at the 1972 Annual Meeting of the American Educational Research Association (ERIC Order No. ED 062 714).

17. The diagnostic team is that unit designated to assist the principal in diagnosing his strengths and weaknesses as an administrator. It may be composed of his immediate supervisor in the school system, one or more of his fellow principals, one or more outside consultants, or other appropriate personnel.

18. For a more complete discussion of these ideas, see Easton, *Systems Analysis.*

19. See Edgar H. Schein, *Professional Education: Some New Directions* (New York: McGraw-Hill, 1972), chs. 8, 9. Schein provides a useful discussion and examples of force-field analysis.

20. See Lawrence and Lorsch, *Organization and Environment.*

21. Andrew W. Halpin, *Theory and Research in Administration* (New York: Macmillan, 1966), pp. 81-130.

22. *Ibid.,* pp. 131-249.

23. This instrument has been adapted from Hemphill, Griffiths, and Frederiksen, *Administrative Performance and Personality.*

FOUR

IMPROVING THE DECISION-MAKING SKILLS OF THE PRINCIPAL

James M. Lipham

Decision making is a central responsibility of the principal. Knowledge about decision making and the application of decision theory should enable the principal to improve his decision-making skills. Assessment of decision-making skills also should benefit school districts in the identification and selection of prospective principals and in the evaluation of practicing principals.[1]

As Gregg indicated, "Decision making is at the very heart of the administrative process."[2] Similarly, McCamy stated, "The reaching of a decision is the core of administration, all other attributes of the administrative process being dependent on, interwoven with, and existent for the making of decisions."[3] Simon also took the view that decision making is synonymous with managing.[4] Earlier, Barnard stated, "The essential process of adaptation in organizations is decision, whereby the physical, biological, personal, and social factors of the situation are selected for specific combination by volitional action."[5] Thus, decision making is a central concern which pervades the entire administrative process since it includes not only a decision, but also the acts necessary to put the decision into operation and so affects the entire course of action of an organization.[6]

In this chapter, a model of the domain, the decision-making process, is presented first. Next, consideration is given to the dimension of decision content—"what" decisions are made by the principal. Decision content is viewed in terms of the problems, tasks, or activities of the principal. Attention is then directed to "how" decisions are made—the decision-making process. The stages in the decision-making process are synthesized and conceptualized according to a systems approach to the modeling of decision behavior. Next, consideration is given to the issue of involvement in decision making—"who" actually makes decisions, as well as "who" ideally should make them. The nature of the principal's involvement in the making of decisions is also considered. The concluding section describes some applications of decision theory to the pre- and in-service training of principals wherein the Atlanta experience is cited as being exemplary.

A MODEL OF THE DECISION-MAKING PROCESS

In considering decision making it is first necessary to define the concept. Here it is defined as a process wherein an awareness of a problematic state of a system, influenced by information and values, is reduced to competing alternatives, among which a choice is made, based upon estimated outcome states of the system. Each of the key concepts involved in this definition—process, problem awareness, information, values, perception, alternatives, choice, and estimated outcomes—is now explained.

Process

Process implies action, that is, a particular set of continuing activities, steps, stages, or operations. Process is always inferred; it is usually sequential, and it is sometimes cyclical. Since process is inferred, it is only an abstraction for the analysis of decision-making behavior. As Halpin cautioned, "An outside observer can never observe 'process' qua 'process,' he can only observe a sequence of behavior or behavior-products from which he may infer process."[7] Thus, in analyzing the decision-making process in the principalship, it is necessary to obtain data from the principal, himself, as well as from observers of the principal's behavior.

In terms of their sequential nature, process formulations are usually conceptualized so that one step serves logically as the basis for the next. In decision making, however, the process may be entered at any stage. The cyclical nature of process also implies that the recurrent steps or stages are recycled in a continual test of the status or attainment of the system at any point in time.[8] In making decisions, the principal often recycles the decision process.

Awareness and Definition of the Problem

Awareness of the problematic state of a system constitutes an initial condition in the decision-making process. Such awareness may range from evident to intuitive, objective to subjective, cognitive to affective, ordered to random, or specific to diffuse. Problem awareness leads to the first systematic stage in the decision-making process, that of classifying and defining the problem. This is a crucial stage since the definition of the problem influences the priority given to it, as well as the selection of a strategy for solving it.

Barnard was among the first to observe that the nature of a problem, in terms of its origin and urgency, is an important consideration in deciding whether one should or should not attempt to solve it. He stated succinctly: "The fine art of executive decision consists of not deciding questions that are not now pertinent, in not deciding prematurely, in not making decisions that cannot be made effective, and in not making decisions that others should make."[9]

Barnard did indicate, however, that three types of decisions may be made: intermediary decisions which originate in authoritative communication from superiors, appellate decisions which stem from cases referred by subordinates, and creative decisions which are initiated by the individual concerned. Recent theorists suggest other bases for analyzing decision making. Delbecq[10] developed a typology that is concerned with the structure of the relationship between individuals, the behavior required to facilitate decision making, the process or manner of proceeding in decision making, and the social-emotional tone of the interpersonal relationship. His categories include routine decision making, heuristic decision making, and compromise decision making.

Routine decision making. Perhaps most of the decisions that a principal makes are routine, whether intermediary or appellate (deriving from above or below him in the organizational hierarchy). In Simon's terms, this is the "programmed" type of decision.[11] That a decision may be routine or programmed does not imply that it is unimportant; it simply indicates that the organization has established the requisite roles and procedures for dealing with the problem. In routine decision making, the situation is usually structured hierarchically (principal to teachers); role behavior is characterized by specialized, yet coordinated effort; the processes utilized are largely formal; the tone of the relationship is likely to be moderately stressful owing to time limitations for action. Many examples come to mind: the principal enforces mandates of the school board, he approves teachers' requisitions, he monitors student attendance, and he interprets disciplinary regulations.

Heuristic decision making. In heuristic or creative decision making there is a lack of emphasis upon hierarchical structure. Role behavior is characterized by each individual being free to explore all ideas bearing upon the problem, and the processes utilized are characterized by full and free discussion. The emotional-social tone is relatively relaxed and characterized by openness and originality. Working with students or teachers in solving a curricular issue is an example of heuristic decision making, particularly if there is no agreed-upon method for dealing with the issue.

Some principals apparently experience difficulty in deciding whether a particular problem should be classified as routine or heuristic. Others, particularly action-oriented principals, are uneasy about utilizing the heuristic mode, even when it is needed. Still others attempt to resolve a problem by vacillating between the modes, as in the case of the principal who calls his staff together and says, "We have a very serious matter here about which I need your help. Now here's how I think we should handle this . . . ."

Compromise decision making. In compromise decision making, also called negotiated decision making, the principal is concerned with a strategy for dealing with conflict, whether because of differences in cultural values, institutional role expectations, or vested interests of individuals. In such situations, one individual or group may stand in opposition to another individual or group concerning either means or ends or both, as, for example, in teacher negotiations. In such situations the group is composed of proportional representation with, ideally, an impartial chairman; role behavior is characterized by each person representing his faction; group processes involve orderly communication, formalized voting procedures, and analytical approaches; and emotional tone may vary from hostility, to candor, to mediation, to conciliation in the desire to reach an agreement or at least an acceptable compromise.

The principal is being called on increasingly to engage in decision making of the compromise type because of conflicts between or within groups: community groups versus the school, teachers versus the board, or one teacher group versus another. Informal observations lead one to suggest that many principals resist unduly the utilization of the compromise decision-making mode. Instead, they continue to depend inappropriately upon routinized or heuristic decision-making techniques. By its very nature, the principalship sometimes demands not only that the principal establish a compromise decision structure, but also that he serve as the impartial mediator in the decision-making process.

The model in Figure 4-1 shows that classification and definition of the problem is the first important stage to be considered in making decisions.

Information

To indicate that information serves as the basis for decision making appears to belabor the obvious, yet three points deserve consideration: amount, form, and flow of information. Regarding amount of information, the analysis of the decision-making behavior of principals has revealed that the search for additional information, whether by communicating with others in writing, by telephone, or in person, logically constitutes an initial stage in preparing to make a decision. The analysis of a decision maker's perceived information needs and information search patterns provides tangible evidence of his decision-making skills. Some principals, for example, erroneously tend to view themselves as gatekeepers of information by "playing it close to the vest"; others tend to utilize only limited data sources or information-gathering procedures; still others engage in "information overload" by obtaining reams of data that may be only tangentially related to the problem at hand. These and other tendencies concerning information search can be readily assessed. Through training, they might also be improved.

Concerning form, information must be more than a mere collection of random data; it must be organized if it is to be useful. Thus, considerable attention is directed within the school to the importance of obtaining information relevant for decision making. Recent-

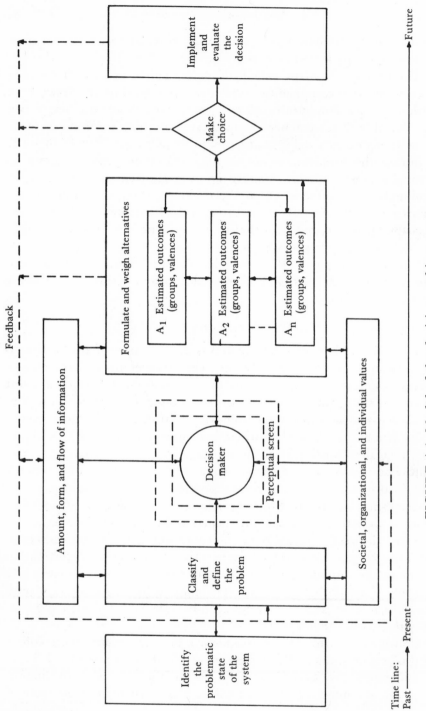

FIGURE 4-1. Model of the decision-making process

Time line:
Past ——→ Present ——→ Future

ly, powerful management information tools and evaluation procedures have been developed which present data in the form that is required.

Finally, concerning flow, information must be made available when it is needed; otherwise it is useless. As shown in Figure 4-1, whereas problem awareness may range from past to present, information bears a present-time relevance for the decision maker. There is a need for responsive channels of communication that foster the flow of information downward, parallel, and upward within the school system and inward and outward with the community.

Values

The values of the society, the organization, and the individual are inextricably entwined in the making of all decisions. The principal's own values serve as a perceptual screen that affects both his awareness of the problem and his screening of information relative to the problem. Values also condition the screening of possible alternatives and the extent to which each alternative will be congruent with the value systems of those affected by a decision. Finally, values serve as the criteria against which higher-order goals are assessed and projected since the principal serves simultaneously as value analyst and value witness in the process of making decisions.

There is a lack of systematic knowledge concerning the relationship of value orientations to decision behavior, and further investigation in this domain is warranted. For example, how do program cost decisions made by a principal who holds a traditional value orientation (save) compare with those of a principal who holds an emergent value orientation (spend)? Or, how do decisions made by a principal who subscribes to the value assumptions of McGregor's Theory Y compare with those made by a principal who subscribes to Theory X?[12] How important to the principal's decision-making behavior is similarity or dissimilarity of values between him and the teachers? Further study is needed, not only of how values relate to decision behavior but also of how values affect decision behavior.

It should also be noted that values interact with rationality in decision making. Heretofore nonrational decision making has been considered primarily a function of incomplete, inaccurate, or untimely information. Yet the model in Figure 4-1 shows that a decision believed to be rational by a decision maker in terms of his value orientations may be judged nonrational, irrational, or even indefensible by those who hold different value orientations. Thus, rationality can also be dependent on value orientations.

Perception

Many factors in addition to values constitute the perceptual screen of the decision maker, and these include such personal variables as intelligence, creativity, need-dispositions, abilities, and even the biological state of the organism. Training and previous experiences also influence the ways in which one cognizes, structures, and perceives the decision situation. Situational or organizational variables, such as who in the formal or informal structure has the "ear" of the decision maker, reputations of others for reliable input, mutual respect for divergent points of view, and the exercise of political or power relationships—all affect the perceptual screen of the decision maker.

As shown in Figure 4-1, the perceptual screen, in a sense, surrounds the decision maker and affects all elements of the decision process, including identifying, classifying, and defining the problem, processing information, estimating value orientations, formulating and weighing alternatives, and making the decision choice. Since one lives and acts in terms of the world as he sees it, the perceptual screen of the decision maker is of great significance.

Competing Alternatives

Competing alternatives represent actions that might be taken or things that might be done to solve the problematic state of a system. Early in the decision process, competing alternatives are typically viewed as substantive in nature, dealing with alternative needs, problems, or opportunities; subsequently, these alternatives become procedural in nature, involving structuring, providing, and assessing possible courses of action to resolve the problem. Formulation of competing alternatives requires consideration of the criteria—validity, reliability, objectivity, relevance, scope, credibility, efficiency, and effectiveness—against which possible outcomes will be assessed.

To say that alternatives are in competition connotes that in most situations the decision maker is faced with conflict, either potential or actual, latent or manifest. Since such conflict may concern goals, roles, or individuals, it is endemic to the decision-making process and particularly evident at the stage of formulating and weighing alternatives. Hence, it is often useful to conceive of decision making as a process of resolving conflict.

In attempting to resolve conflict concerning competing alternatives, it is frequently deemed necessary to collect additional data. Collection of additional data alone does not, however, enable one to make a decision; it can even complicate rather than facilitate the process.

Choice

Selecting a solution strategy from among decision alternatives is termed the decision choice, and it involves judging the outcomes or consequences of each decision alternative and selecting that solution deemed most likely to reduce the problematic state. This stage in the process is often an individualistic or personalistic matter, although through formal organizational or informal group processes agreement on the choice may cause it to be termed an organizational or a collaborative decision.

Some have tended to equate the "moment of choice" with the entire decision-making process; it is, however, only one stage, albeit a crucial one, where the decision maker weighs the maximum input-outcome relationships. At this point the decision maker assesses each decision alternative and estimates the probable outcomes of each until a choice is made.

Regarding the timing of the decision choice, there also are decision skills that can be practiced and learned. Some principals apparently are able to evaluate alternatives more quickly and accurately than others; they can make crucial decisions, even in rapid-fire order. Others take considerable time to make a choice, even engaging in decision-avoidance behavior in the hope that they will not ultimately need to make a choice. Time is spent, perhaps, seeking additional information, attempting to formulate additional alternatives, or reformulating the nature of the problem. Since the decision-making process is time-bound, however, it must be realized that even the decision not to decide is also an alternative.

Estimated Outcomes

Estimation of the outcome state of a system involves posing the issue, "If this, then what?"

As Bross stressed, for each decision alternative the consequences can be predicted only in terms of a probable, rather than a certain, chain of events.[13] In schools, some of the factors to be estimated include the nature and number of individuals or groups for which the decision is relevant, the degree to which each individual or group is affected by the decision, and the way in which each individual or group perceives the decision. Again, communication of information and perception of the value orientations of others are crucial considerations for school principals since their decisions usually concern people rather than things.

"WHAT" DECISIONS ARE MADE: DECISION CONTENT

Although it is possible to conceive of decision making in the abstract, decisions always relate to the major substantive content of a focal role—"what" decisions are to be made. In the case of the school principal, such substantive content, typically termed the functions or tasks of the principal, may be categorized as: curriculum and instruction, staff personnel, student personnel, financial and physical resources, and school-community relations.

Other categorizations have also been utilized to analyze the principalship.[14] It is possible, moreover, to focus either upon "balance" among the five categories or, depending upon the nature of problems within the school,[15] to focus upon only one category, such as the improvement of instruction.[16] It is then possible to analyze the tasks or functions performed by the principal within a category.

Decision Role Analysis

An approach to describing the principalship that is somewhat different from task analysis is that of decision role analysis—defining the principalship in terms of the major decisions that rest with the position. This approach possesses certain advantages over the task approach in that it is possible not only to indicate which decisions fall within the province of the role, but also to specify decision expectations held by the principal, himself, decision expectations held by the teachers for him, and his perceptions of the decision expectations held by the teachers. Examination of the relationships among these three sets of data is meaningful.

Expectations for a role incumbent's behavior are obtained through a process of decision role analysis. The expectations range from required to prohibited: the principal "absolutely must" (5), "probably should" (4), "may or may not" (3), "probably should not" (2), or "absolutely must not" (1) either make the decisions or display the behavior described regarding the decisions. Sample instruments for conducting a decision (Content) Role Analysis are shown in Figure 4-2. Other terms, such as, "always" (5), "often" (4), "sometimes" (3), "seldom" (2), or "never" (1), may be used to establish a full range relating to the decision. Another useful method for analyzing decision expectations is that of requiring respondents to rank or sort decision items, one against the other, in order of importance. Still another method requires an assessment of the time allotted to decision items through analysis of a principal's calendar or by observations of his on-the-job behavior.

Regardless of the methodologies utilized, two types of useful data may be obtained: the "real" or actual decision role of the principal, and the "idealized" or preferred decision role of the principal. Difference scores or discrepancy comparisons between the real and the ideal are often revealing. In the case of the principal, himself, the difference between his actual decision behavior and the idealized decision behavior that he posits for his position is considered to be a derived measure of role adequacy. In the case of others, such as teachers, the difference between the decision behavior that the principal actually exhibits as contrasted with the behavior that they ideally would like to see him exhibit is considered to be a derived measure of their perceived effectiveness of the principal.

Decision Expectations and Perceptions

The complementary principal-teacher relationship can be used to depict the three types of decision expectations—the principal's own expectations, the teachers' expectations for him, and his perceptions of the teachers' expectations for him—and interactions between and among them. In Figure 4-3, which deals only with actual rather than ideal expectations, point A in the model relates to one's own decision expectations. In obtaining this set of expectations a list of decisions is presented to the respondent, in this case the principal, in terms of the prompt, "As principal, I make the decision on . . . ." or "As principal, I am expected to make the decision on . . . ." Utilizing a similar procedure, one also can obtain a measure of the principal's ideal decision-making role. To do this, the prompt utilized is, "Ideally, as principal, I should make the decision on . . . ." Many principals believe that introspective analysis alone, that is, comparing their actual with their idealized decision-making roles, is a particularly

DECISION (CONTENT) ROLE ANALYSIS SCALE
Principal's Form (actual)

As principal, I am expected to make the decision on (sample items from the Atlanta form):	Absolutely must	Probably should	May or may not	Probably should not	Absolutely must not
1. Teacher absenteeism and utilization of sick leave	5	4	3	2	1
2. The standards for student dress and conduct	5	4	3	2	1
3. The selection and employment of new teachers	5	4	3	2	1
4. The curricular innovations to be attempted in the school	5	4	3	2	1
5. The appointment of citizens to advisory councils	5	4	3	2	1
6. Other, including locally determined decision content items					

Principal's Form (ideal)

Ideally, as principal, I should make the decision on:					
1. Teacher absenteeism and utilization of sick leave	5	4	3	2	1
2. Etc.					

Teacher's Form (actual)

I expect my principal to make the decision on:					
1. Teacher absenteeism and utilization of sick leave	5	4	3	2	1
2. Etc.					

Teacher's Form (ideal)

Ideally, my principal should make the decisions on:					
1. Teacher absenteeism and utilization of sick leave	5	4	3	2	1
2. Etc.					

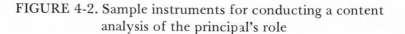

FIGURE 4-2. Sample instruments for conducting a content analysis of the principal's role

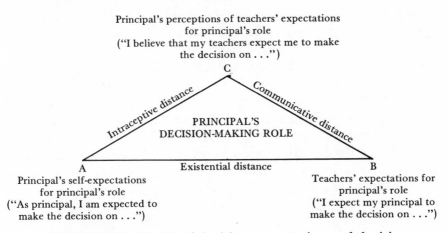

Principal's perceptions of teachers' expectations
for principal's role
("I believe that my teachers expect me to make
the decision on . . .")

C

Intraceptive distance

Communicative distance

PRINCIPAL'S
DECISION-MAKING ROLE

A   Existential distance   B

Principal's self-expectations   Teachers' expectations for
for principal's role   principal's role
("As principal, I am expected to   ("I expect my principal to
make the decision on . . .")   make the decision on . . .")

FIGURE 4-3. Model of decision-expectation and decision-
perception relationships

valuable and worthwhile experience in that it pinpoints areas of discrepancy to which they may direct greater attention.

Others' expectations, in this case the teachers at point B in Figure
4-3, may be obtained by administering the same list of decision items
to the teachers preceded by the prompt, "I expect my principal to
make the decision on . . . ." Thus, the difference between the principal's own expectations and the expectations held for him by the
teachers may be documented and computed. From analyzing an entire series of decision content categories or items, a measure of agreement or consensus, or, conversely, disagreement or conflict potential,
may be obtained in both direction and magnitude.

Line AB between point A in Figure 4-3, the principal's own expectations, and point B, the teachers' expectations, represents basic
philosophical differences that may be caused by differences between
principals and teachers on such variables as training, group membership, hierarchical organizational position, role empathy, previous experiences, and myriad other factors. The length of line AB represents
the role distance between the principal and the teachers; it may range
from complete agreement to complete disagreement. In Figure 4-3,
therefore, line AB has been labeled *existential distance*.

In addition to the direct differences in decision expectations held
by the principal, himself, point A, and those held by the teachers for

the principal, point B, disagreements and misunderstanding also can derive from another source, point C in Figure 4-3. Such differences are not existential, but perceptual. That is, the principal may believe that he and his teachers hold significant differences in their expectations when, in fact, they are the same; conversely, he may believe they are the same when, in fact, they are different. To obtain the measure of one's perceptions of others' role expectations, such prompts as the following are used, "I feel (think, believe, or perceive) that my teachers expect me to make the decision on. . . ." Again, the same list of decision items may be used to obtain comparable data.

Line AC in Figure 4-3 is termed *intraceptive distance*. Regarding this distance, two points should be made. First, research on perception has revealed that, more often than not, there is a systematic tendency for one to perceive the expectations of others to be closer to his own than, in fact, they are. This tendency seems to hold whether it is role, value, or even personality variables that are being perceived. Second, intraception is composed of both need and ability components, either of which can be altered through experience or training.

Some observations should also be made concerning the difference or distance between what teachers actually expect and what the principal thinks they expect. This difference, line BC in Figure 4-3, has been labeled *communicative distance*. Most studies of organizational roles have revealed that ineffectiveness and inefficiency are due less to differences that are out in the open and understood than to those that are underground and misunderstood. Thus, the procedure outlined permits principal and teachers to discuss freely and openly their mutual expectations for each other's decision-making roles, thereby reducing the communicative distance between complementary organizational role incumbents.

Utilizing the same decision content items, one also can rate the effectiveness of the principal's decision-making behavior for each category and for each item. It is desirable to separate descriptions of behavior from evaluations of the quality of that behavior. Evaluative ratings may be self-ratings by the principal or ratings by significant other groups utilizing the prompt, "The principal's effectiveness in making the decision on . . . is _____ ."

Studies of the decision content of the principal's role are subject to all of the limitations of role studies, including interdependence of the data, mistaking disagreement for conflict, presuming disagreement somehow to be "bad," failing to control for the size of the respondent group, and ignoring the difficulty in estimating the expectations of a group. Even so, base line data concerning "what" decisions the principal makes are necesssary for improving relationships between the principal and those with whom he must deal daily.

"HOW" DECISIONS ARE MADE: DECISION BEHAVIOR

A systems approach is useful for analyzing "how" decisions are made. Within the systems approach to decision making, the process may be viewed according to two major categories of behavior: system analysis and system synthesis. As shown in Figure 4-4, system analysis includes two steps: identifying the nature of the problem, and determining solution requirements and alternatives. System synthesis involves the remaining three steps: choosing a solution strategy from alternatives, implementing the solution strategy, and determining performance effectiveness.[17] System design or system modeling includes all five steps. In a systems approach, each of the steps, including some tools and techniques useful to the principal, must be considered (see Figure 4-4). Most principals already are generally familiar with the steps, since they approximate the stages in the scientific method.

Identifying the Problem

Whether through programmed situations or the assessment of unmet needs and emerging opportunities, becoming aware that a decision is needed is a basic element in the decision-making process.[18] As indicated earlier, many decisions made by principals are programmed or routinized in nature. If roles are mutually understood and if decision responsibilities are clearly affixed, as stressed in the preceding section, such problems present little difficulty to principals in terms of identifying the decision.

The assessment of unmet needs provides another means for identifying the problem. In systems terms a need may be defined as a problem created because of a discrepancy that should not exist.[19] The discrepancy can be between groups concerning a particular variable (for example, Miss Jones's students on reading versus Miss Smith's students on reading), or between the actual state ("what is") and the

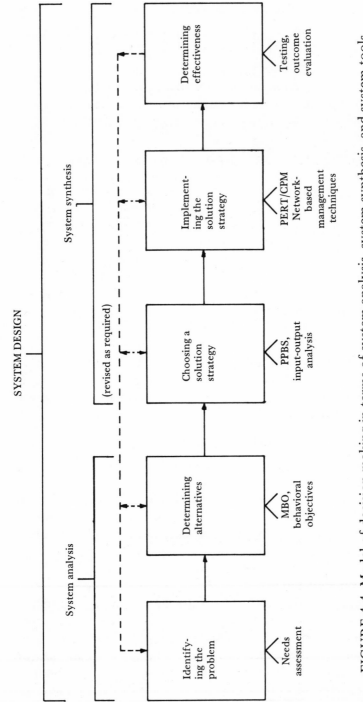

FIGURE 4-4. Model of decision making in terms of system analysis, system synthesis, and system tools for the improvement of education. *Source*: Adapted from Roger A. Kaufman, "System Approaches to Education: Discussion and Attempted Integration," in Philip K. Piele, Terry L. Eidell, and Stuart C. Smith (eds.), *Social and Technological Change: Implications for Education* (Eugene: Center for Advanced Study of Educational Administration, University of Oregon, 1970), pp. 143, 168.

idealized state ("what should be"). For example, we may feel that no student in the school is being trained to be an "independent learner," which, of itself, may represent an educational need.[20] Once educational needs have been expressed in terms of discrepancies, it is possible to generate measurable objectives by stating them as the reduction of needs over time.

Under conditions of scarce or limited resources, the principal must select the problem area that represents the greatest discrepancy or the most urgent need. While a needs assessment may start with symptoms or problems, it subsequently translates them into goals and objectives. Such objectives and goals preferably should be stated in terms of performance or behavior, rather than in terms of process.[21] Through conducting a systematic needs assessment, the principal will be able to isolate significant problems and to design alternative solutions.

Determining Alternatives

The second stage of decision making, formulating solution requirements and alternatives, involves the following:[22]
1. Conducting a four-stage mission analysis
   a. Identifying an overall mission objective: "Where are we going?"
   b. Determining constraints: "What are the things that will keep us from where we are going?"
   c. Removing constraints: "How do we eliminate those things that keep us from where we are going?"
   d. Preparing a mission profile: "What are the milestones along the way to where we are going?"
2. Performing function and task analysis: "What specifically must be done to get to each milestone?"
3. Performing function and task analysis: "What are the possible alternatives of getting each function and task done?"
4. Formulating the criteria to be used in assessing alternatives.
5. Formulating the decision rules for selecting an alternative.

At the school level, the utilization of management by objectives (MBO) and, at the classroom level, the specification of behavioral objectives are tools that are useful in this stage of decision making. Included in the objectives are specifications of what is to be done, by whom, under what conditions, and in terms of which criteria.

Choosing a Solution Strategy

The third stage in the decision-making process is that of choosing a solution strategy from among the alternatives. It involves:

1. Obtaining and assessing information related to each decision alternative.
2. Applying the decision rules to the available evidence. (This may be straightforward and unambiguous or highly subjective and intuitive.)
3. Choosing one alternative.
4. Reflecting on the efficacy of the indicated choice.
5. Confirming the indicated choice or rejecting it. (The decision maker also may seek more information, change the decision rules, formulate additional alternatives, or choose the alternative in use by default.)[23]

Three quantitative management tools—management information systems, planning-programming-budgeting systems, and input-output (cost-effectiveness, cost-benefit, or cost-utility) analysis—are particularly useful at this stage since each is designed to maximize the "wisdom" of the decision maker. Management information systems provide specific, instantaneous data along relevant dimensions concerning past and current system performance and thereby provide the necessary comparative information essential for an intelligent choice among alternatives. Planning-programming-budgeting systems permit examination of the relative merits of alternatives by projecting programs into the future and by indicating the financial requirements of each program. Input-output analysis provides a means for examining alternatives by directly raising the questions, "What do I give?" "What do I get?" Even if such tools simply array the available information, they help to sharpen the judgment of the principal in choosing a solution strategy from the various alternatives.

Implementing the Solution Strategy

At the implementation stage, even the best decision may founder. To monitor implementation of the solution strategy, two types of process evaluation, implementation evaluation and progress evaluation, are necessary. Implementation evaluation is designed to assess the extent to which the solution strategy actually is being carried out in the intended manner. Typical questions might be: "Did the supplies arrive on time?" "Are the students who are enrolled the ones for whom the program was intended?" or "Do the teachers have the qualifications needed to conduct the program?"[24] Such information is useful to the principal in deciding whether it is appropriate to allow the program to continue as it is presently operating or to recycle the decision process.

Progress evaluation, on the other hand, is aimed at determining whether or not the program is actually making gains toward achieving its objectives. A program may be implemented exactly as planned, but still not reach its intended objectives. It would be wasteful to install a program in the fall and have to wait until spring to learn that it had failed and that corrective action might have made it work. Principals need information about progress during the course of a program so that problems, if they develop, can be identified and corrected quickly. Progress evaluation provides information on how a program is functioning relative to short-range objectives, as well as information concerning unforeseen or unanticipated outcomes valuable to the principal in making decisions.[25]

Several management tools designed to monitor program implementation are useful in both of these types of process evaluation. One example is flow charting, which permits a synthesis of both the elements of the system and the operations that the system performs. It is particularly useful in conceptualizing the relationship of functions to objectives. Another example is network analysis, which includes program evaluation review technique and critical path method. Such analyses are particularly valuable in that they show not only what is happening in an overall effort, but also how each part affects all the other parts. Both flow charting and network analysis highlight in interactive fashion the major and minor decisions that must be made.

Determining Effectiveness

The final stage in the systems approach to "how" decisions are made is that of determining the general worth of the implemented solution. This judgment, often called program certification, is based on outcome evaluations concerning the extent to which objectives have been achieved.[26] Outcome evaluation deals with such questions as: "Shall we extend the program to third-graders as well as to second-graders?" "Shall the program be tried in different subject fields?" "Should we continue the program next year?" Norm-referenced and criterion-referenced tests are the most obvious techniques for determining performance effectiveness and answering such questions, although a variety of evaluative methods and instruments may be used.

As in the case of measuring decision role content, it is possible to obtain real and ideal measures of the frequency of decision process behavior. A sample instrument for analyzing the decision process behavior of the principal is shown in Figure 4-5. In many ways this

DECISION (PROCESS) BEHAVIOR ANALYSIS
(Principal's Form)

In making decisions I . . . (sample items only)	Always	Often	Some-times	Seldom	Never
1. Identify the emotional elements of a problem	5	4	3	2	1
2. Seek alternative solutions from others	5	4	3	2	1
3. Determine who will be affected by each alternative	5	4	3	2	1
4. Gain support for my decisions	5	4	3	2	1
5. Allow others to implement decisions	5	4	3	2	1
6. Seek unique alternative solutions	5	4	3	2	1
7. Compute the costs of various alternatives	5	4	3	2	1
8. Maintain feedback mechanisms, etc.	5	4	3	2	1
	5	4	3	2	1

FIGURE 4-5. Sample instrument for analyzing the decision-making behavior of the principal

procedure is analogous to that utilized in the assessment of leadership behavior; therefore, the items used to measure decision process behavior are generalizable and not confined to one school district or school. Such measures may also be used to obtain the principal's perceptions of others' responses. The utilization of outside observers or in-basket exercises are other means for measuring the frequency with which a principal engages in certain of the decision process behaviors.

Again, it is possible, through changing the prompt and response sets, to utilize the same decision process behavior items to obtain ratings of the perceived effectiveness of one's decision-making behavior.

"WHO" MAKES DECISIONS: DECISION INVOLVEMENT

A major complication in the analysis of decision making in a complex organization such as a school is that decisions are shared, that is, more than one role incumbent is typically involved in the process, and such involvement may also be differential in nature. In examining the sharing of decisions, a procedure known as decision involvement analysis is useful.[27] In analyzing decision involvement, the major items are derived in terms of local needs as in decision (content) role analysis, although a standard list of decisions dealing with such functions as curriculum, staff personnel, student personnel, finance, and school-community relations may be utilized. Next, a list of specific position titles ranging from the board of education to students is identified. A sample format for the decision involvement analysis instrument developed for the Atlanta Public Schools is shown in Figure 4-6. Question 1 provides data on the respondents' perceptions of who actually makes each decision. Question 2 provides data on the respondents' ideal perceptions—who should make each decision. When data are obtained from respondents at all organizational levels, it becomes possible to compare perceptions of the actual with the ideal decision-making structure of the organization.

The nature of one's own involvement in the decision-making process may range from high to low, as follows:

5. Make the decision
4. Recommend an alternative
3. Develop possible alternatives
2. Provide information only
1. No involvement

Utilizing the decision involvement analysis instrument, each respondent is also able to specify the actual (Question 3) and the ideal (Question 4) nature of his own involvement in each decision. Again, it is possible to make meaningful comparisons between the actual and the ideal. Such studies have revealed, for example, that principals may be deeply involved in making some decisions that they do not care to make, yet they may be only minimally involved in making some decisions that they do wish to make.

In analyzing decision involvement it also may be desirable to add consideration of frequency or "how often" a person is involved in

DECISION INVOLVEMENT ANALYSIS
(Principal's form—Atlanta schools)

Questions

Please answer these four questions in terms of your school or school system by placing the appropriate number of the response in the boxes provided for each decision item. Place only one answer in each box.

1. Which person or persons are *primarily responsible* at the present time for making this decision?

2. Which person or persons do you believe *should be primarily responsible* for making this decision?

3. What is the *present nature* of your involvement in making this decision?

4. What do you believe *should be the nature* of your involvement in making this decision?

Sample Item:

Selection and employment of new teachers

1. [5]

2. [6]

3. [4]

4. [5]

Responses for questions 1 and 2

The person or persons primarily responsible for making the decision:

1—Board of education
2—Superintendent of schools
3—Assistant superintendent
4—Area superintendent
5—Director (system-wide)
6—Principal
7—Assistant principal
8—Coordinator or resource teacher
9—Department head or unit leader
10—Teacher
11—Student

Responses for questions 3 and 4

Nature of your involvement in the decision-making process:

5—Make the decision
4—Recommend an alternative
3—Develop possible alternatives
2—Provide information
1—No involvement

FIGURE 4-6. Sample instrument for analyzing involvement in decision making

decision making to the response format, as well as to obtain a measure of the mechanisms for involvement. It is possible, by listing various group structures—the ubiquitous cabinets, councils, and committees in school systems—as well as position levels, to obtain data and analyze mechanisms utilized for involvement in decision making.

Analyses of involvement in decision making generally have uncovered considerable disagreement in perceptions of decision-making structures in schools. Moreover, the extent of such disagreement has been shown to relate to meaningful organizational variables, such as curricular change, and to individual variables, such as training and experience. Finally, results of the studies of decision involvement have been particularly useful in clarifying or altering the decision-making structure of schools and school districts.

APPLICATION OF DECISION THEORY

Decision making was defined, within the context of a systems approach, as a process wherein an awareness of a problematic state of a system, influenced by information and values, is reduced to competing alternatives, among which a choice is made, based upon estimated outcome states of the system. Three dimensions—decision content, decision behavior, and decision involvement—were posited as useful and necessary for assessing or improving the school principal's decision-making role and skills. Relationships among the three dimensions are depicted in Figure 4-7.

Although the dimensions are conceptually independent, in practice they are usually examined in viable combinations: decision content with decision behavior, decision content with decision involvement, or decision behavior with decision involvement. Moreover, it is possible, and often desirable, to focus upon only one or some of the problems, rather than all of the problems within the dimensions. For example, a principal's involvement in finance and business management decisions might be quite clear, in contrast to his involvement in curriculum and instruction decisions. Finally, one, some, or all of the factors within the dimensions or the cells within Figure 4-7 might be examined in relation to other important organizational or individual variables.

In utilizing or applying existing knowledge of theory and research on decision making, several activity modes are available to school

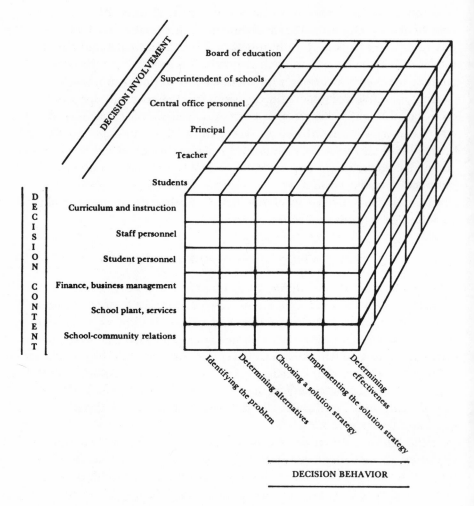

FIGURE 4-7. Three basic dimensions of the principal's
decision-making role

systems, including developmental, assessment, interactive, and structural change modes.

Developmental Mode

The major thrust of the developmental mode in the application of decision theory is to build, design, or adapt instrumentation concerning decision making that is system specific or unique to the problems, procedures, or issues in the local educational agency. In Atlanta, for example, representative groups of principals and central office administrators met to define and delimit the following:

1. The major decision content categories and decision items, appropriate to the principal's role, that should be included in the decision role analysis scale. Moreover, attention was given to the selection of prompts and of response sets suitable for inclusion on the scale.
2. The general behavioral items that should be adapted or modified to be included on the decision behavior analysis scale.
3. The major decision content items and the school district positions to be included on the decision involvement analysis scale.

During the developmental mode in the Atlanta project, consideration was given to whether all or only some of the dimensions of decision making were to be attacked simultaneously. Attention was also directed toward determining the desirability and feasibility of obtaining data concerning decisions that the principal actually makes or decisions that he ideally should make. In Atlanta, it was decided that both should be assessed.

Such developmental activities possess considerable merit in that they focus meaningfully and critically not only upon the principal's decision-making role but also upon the decision structure of the entire school system. Not to be overlooked is the ancillary benefit that, through the process of engaging in developmental activities, the primary participants gain considerable understanding of decision theory as they seek to operationalize the assessment of decision content, decision behavior, and decision involvement.

Assessment Mode

The major thrust of the assessment mode to the application of decision theory is both organizationally and individually diagnostic. In the assessment process, data are obtained from the principal and from organizational superiors and subordinates concerning the real or ideal decision role, behavior, and involvement. In Atlanta, for example, consideration was given to administering the decision role analysis, decision behavior analysis, and decision involvement analysis scales to measure:

1. The principal's expectations concerning his decision role, behavior, and involvement;
2. The district administrators' and supervisors' expectations concerning the principal's decision role, behavior, and involvement;
3. The teachers' expectations concerning the principal's decision role, behavior, and involvement.

When analyzed by district, the resultant data highlight the decision-making aspects of the principalship role within the school organization. When analyzed by school, the data possess particular significance for the individual principal who is thereby enabled to engage in a penetrating introspective analysis of his decision making.

Interactive Mode

The interactive mode is designed to improve the individual principal's decision-making skills. It is appropriate for structuring a wide variety of in-service training and preservice selection activities concerning decision making. Utilizing data from the assessment mode, for example, groups of principals could hold meaningful in-service meetings at the district level to review and interpret the findings. Similarly, the findings by school can serve as a basis for constructive in-service meetings of each principal with his teachers.

Several school systems have utilized simulation training materials to diagnose and improve the decision-making skills of school principals. Such workshops could be conducted during which the principal's decision making on the simulation exercises is scored using, for example, the decision behavior analysis scale. Many instructive comparisons can be made between the principal's decision behavior during simulation with his decision behavior on the job. Other exciting interactive procedures, such as peer assessment of decision behavior, computer scoring of decision behavior, and structured observations of decision behavior, can be utilized to provide the practicing principal with immediate feedback concerning his decision-making skills.

In selecting school principals, some leading school districts have found it desirable to have applicants and nominees for promotion to the principalship engage in exercises wherein attention is focused specifically on decision making. As a part of these exercises, assessments are made of such important personalistic variables as value orientations, information search patterns, and range and quality of alternatives developed, as well as assessments of the dimensions of decision role, behavior, and involvement. Data from such measures serve to augment and sharpen considerably the traditional criteria utilized for making appointments to the principalship.

Structural Change Mode

Whereas the interactive mode is personalistic in nature, the structural change mode is concerned with specifying or modifying the decision structure of the organization as a result of activities pertaining to the three previously described modes. In a sense, it represents a return to the developmental mode, but armed with data from the assessment mode and fortified by changes within individuals as a result of the interactive mode.

In the structural mode, attention is focused upon changing the organizational decision structure, clarifying role and position descriptions, reconciling conflicts in the decision structure, altering decision involvement patterns and relationships, and similar activities designed to increase the degree of congruence both between the real and the ideal and between the organization and the individual.

The decision to conduct a program designed to improve the decision-making skills of school principals is high in potency and requires considerable commitment of personnel and other resources. School systems that have used the four modes, however, report substantial gain in both organizational and individual performance. This is the goal toward which decision theory should be applied.

NOTES

1. Portions of this paper are drawn from: James M. Lipham and James A. Hoeh, Jr., *The Principalship: Foundations and Functions* (New York: Harper & Row, 1974), chs. 2, 6, 7.

2. Russell T. Gregg, "The Administrative Process," in Roald F. Campbell and Russell T. Gregg (eds.), *Administrative Behavior in Education* (New York: Harper & Row, 1957), p. 275.

3. James L. McCamy, "An Analysis of the Process of Decision Making," *Public Administration Review*, 7 (Winter 1947), 41.

4. Herbert A. Simon, *The New Science of Management Decision* (New York: Harper & Row, 1960).

5. Chester I. Barnard, *The Functions of the Executive* (Cambridge, Mass.: Harvard University Press, 1938), p. 286.

6. Daniel E. Griffiths, *Administrative Theory* (New York: Appleton-Century-Crofts, 1959), p. 76.

7. Andrew W. Halpin, "A Paradigm for Research on Administrative Behavior," in Roald F. Campbell and Russell T. Gregg (eds.), *Administrative Behavior in Education* (New York: Harper & Row, 1957), p. 195.

8. Phi Delta Kappa National Study Committee on Evaluation, *Educational Evaluation and Decision Making* (Itasca, Ill.: Peacock, 1971), p. 83.

9. Barnard, *Functions of the Executive,* p. 194.

10. Andrae L. Delbecq, "The Management of Decision-Making within the Firm: Three Strategies for Three Types of Decision Making," *Academy of Management Journal,* 10 (December 1967), 329-339.

11. Simon, *New Science of Management Decision,* pp. 5-20.

12. See Douglas McGregor, *The Human Side of Enterprise* (New York: McGraw-Hill, 1960), pp. 33-57. (Theory Y views behavior in terms of human growth, self-direction, and self-fulfillment; Theory X, in terms of organization, direction, and control.)

13. Irwin D. J. Bross, *Design for Decision* (New York: Macmillan, 1953), pp. 25-26.

14. See Robert E. Greene, *Administrative Appraisal: A Step to Improved Leadership* (Washington, D. C.: National Association of Secondary School Principals, 1972), pp. 30-32.

15. Such problems and issues are best specified by personnel working in the environment, e.g., Atlanta principals, in this instance.

16. See Chapter Six.

17. Roger A. Kaufman, "Systems Approaches to Education: Discussion and Attempted Integration," in Philip K. Piele, Terry L. Eidell, and Stuart C. Smith (eds.), *Social and Technological Changes: Implications for Education* (Eugene, Ore.: Center for the Advanced Study of Educational Administration, University of Oregon, 1970), pp. 162-163.

18. Phi Delta Kappa National Study Committee on Evaluation, *Educational Evaluation and Decision Making,* p. 52.

19. John M. Gottman and Robert E. Clasen, *Evaluation in Education* (Itasca, Ill.: Peacock, 1972), p. 46.

20. *Ibid.*

21. Stephen Klein, Gary Fenstermacher, and Marvin C. Alkin, "The Center's Changing Evaluation Model," *Evaluation Comment* (Center for the Study of Evaluation, University of California, Los Angeles), 2 (January 1971), 9.

22. Kaufman, "Systems Approaches to Education," p. 148; Phi Delta Kappa National Study Committee on Evaluation, *Educational Evaluation and Decision Making,* p. 53.

23. *Ibid.*

24. Klein, Fenstermacher, and Alkin, "Center's Changing Evaluation Model."

25. *Ibid.,* p. 12.

26. Marvin C. Alkin, "Evaluation Theory Development," *Evaluation Comment,* 2 (October 1969), 5.

27. Gordon E. Wendlandt, "Faculty Involvement in the Decision-Making Process and Experience in Collective Negotiations," doctoral dissertation, University of Wisconsin, 1970.

FIVE

ACHIEVING EFFECTIVE HUMAN RELATIONS AND MORALE

Larry W. Hughes

Few administrative acts are performed that do not affect people. Good human relations are, therefore, critical to the success of an enterprise, and the effective use of human resources in an organization requires good interpersonal relations, a serious consideration in any administrative process. One of the major roles which a principal has is to deploy and develop human resources. The effectiveness with which this is done also depends in great part on good interpersonal relations.

Because any school system is an example of social interaction, certain assumptions can be made:

1. The principal is a key actor;
2. The individual school provides the locus of a primary social group;[1]
3. The reason for examining social interaction in a school is to provide a more effective means to achieve organizational goals.

Asch maintains that "to act in the social field requires a knowledge of social forces—of persons and groups. To take our place with

The writer is indebted to Mrs. Harriet Crump, graduate assistant in the Department of Educational Administration and Supervision at the University of Tennessee, for assistance in preparing this manuscript.

others we must perceive each other's existence and reach a measure of comprehension of one another's needs, emotions, and thoughts."[2]

THE MULTIFUNCTIONAL ORGANIZATION

Most theoretical models support the view that a formal organization such as a school is multifunctional. In order to be effective, that is, in order for the goals of an organization to be achieved, it devotes a part of its resources to such functions as the creation of further means to the goal, the maintenance of units performing goal activities, and the social integration of these units.

A public school organization secures the support of a community by stating that the intellectual development of students is a major goal. Part of its resources are devoted to this goal, but some resources must also be devoted to the personal needs satisfaction of the organizational members. These may not be directly related; indeed, they may at times prevent achieving the stated goals of the organization.

Etzioni[3] argues persuasively from this perspective. He maintains that a proper goal model for determining organizational effectiveness would show that the organization has different goals from the ones it claims to have, particularly those stated publicly. The public goals are intended to enlist the support of the public for the organization; support which, in all probability, would not be forthcoming for its private goals. The private goals—organizational maintenance, service and custodial functions—are, however, just as essential to the continuing existence and effectiveness of the organization as the public goals. If an organization were to invest all of its resources in the realization of its public goals, there could be a complete breakdown of the system so that even the attainment of public goals would be unlikely.

Getzels takes account of the multidimensional nature of organizations when he conceptualizes nomothetic and idiographic dimensions.[4] The administrator's role in this concept is to mediate between the dimensions and to harmonize potentially conflicting forces in the organization (see Figure 5-1).

There is a need not only for task accomplishment within the organization but also for personal satisfaction for those working in it. The more a chief administrator can relate individual needs of an organization and task accomplishment needs of the organization, the more likely the organization is to move toward its goals.[6]

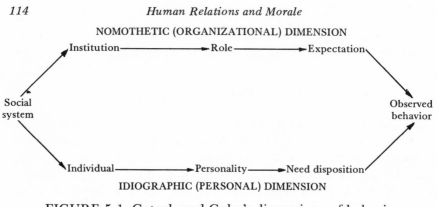

FIGURE 5-1. Getzels and Guba's dimensions of behavior in organizations[5]

Getzels and Guba[7] set forth these ideas quite clearly. Administration, according to the Getzels-Guba model, is conceived as a hierarchy of subordinate-superordinate relationships within a social system that allocates and integrates roles and facilities so that the goals of the system (organization) may be realized. There are two dimensions to such a system: the nomothetic consists of the institution, its official roles, and its expectations; the idiographic consists of the individual, his personality, and his need-dispositions.

The role of the principal in such a social system is that of mediator between the institutional demands on him and his co-workers and the orientations and needs of individual staff members. Such a role requires the development of appropriate interpersonal skills to create good human relations and morale.

Dale Carnegie and others have capitalized on this knowledge, and yet their approach, effective perhaps in a superficial or temporal situation, is of questionable efficacy in a more permanent one.[8] It is doubtful if the administrator can maintain effective working relations if his interest and concern for others is limited to a prescribed pattern of situational behaviors (for example, "move forward when talking to groups"; "maintain eye contact"; "remember names"; "have a hearty handshake"). Such adoptive behavior might suffice for a time, but, if it does not reflect a person's true feelings, it will eventually emerge as deceptive behavior. When interpersonal or human relations are examined as a domain of administrative behavior, a major issue is, therefore, one of personal "authenticity."[9] In authentic relationships the individual enhances his sense of self- and other-awareness and self- and other-acceptance in a way that permits others to do the same. The individual is, in other words, what he appears to be.

The creation of an organizational climate in which active leadership can emerge easily from any source is desirable. This discussion centers on the ability of the principal to deal with others in such a way that he and they can initiate and consummate acts of leadership. Basic to the creation of such a climate and to the development of effective human relations would seem to be the principal's assumptions about those with whom he works. If a principal sees his fellow workers—whether they be teachers, supervisors, custodians, or students—as drone-like, lazy, requiring close supervision, and unresponsive, patterns of interpersonal behavior will likely manifest these assumptions. A hearty handshake and a pat on the back will probably not disguise such assumptions for long.

ASSUMPTIONS ABOUT PEOPLE

Several years ago, Douglas McGregor identified two sets of assumptions—Theory X and Theory Y—which one may hold about people.[10] Theory X, the conventional view of management, is the theory upon which most of the activities of managers (administrators) are based. The theory suggests that man, inherently, does not like to work (or is not competent to direct himself) and that he will avoid work unless there are many formal organizational constraints. Such a philosophy would produce a system of close supervision with strict control over individual behavior. Coercion and threat can be used in a "hard management" approach, but they are not the only methods that can be used. "Soft management" can also result from Theory X assumptions. The approach would be permissive, with emphasis on satisfying low-level employee demands and achieving harmony. If a "boss" is permissive, he believes that, when these goals have been achieved, workers will then behave and accept orders. In either instance, hard or soft, the assumptions are the same: unless workers are coaxed or coerced, they will not behave in a way that will be productive for the organization.

With Theory Y, on the other hand, it is assumed that people are capable of self-direction, and, if given the opportunity along with the appropriate reward system, they will contribute to the achievement of organizational goals.

The administrator's task, based on these two sets of assumptions, can be summarized as follows:

Theory X

1. The administrator is responsible for organizing the elements of productive enterprise—money, materials, equipment, people—in the interest of the goals of the enterprise.
2. With respect to people, this is a process of directing their efforts, motivating them, controlling their actions, and modifying their behavior to fill the needs of the organization.
3. Without this active intervention by the administration, people would be passive, even resistant, to organizational needs. They must, therefore, be persuaded, rewarded, punished, and controlled; their activities must be directed. The administrator's task is managing workers. It is often summed up by saying that administration consists of getting things done through other people.
4. The average man is by nature indolent; he works as little as possible.

Theory Y

1. The administrator is responsible for organizing the elements of productive enterprise—money, materials, equipment, people—in the interest of the goals of the enterprise.
2. People are not by nature passive or resistant to organizational needs. They have become so as a result of experience in organizations.
3. The motivation, the potential for development, the capacity for assuming responsibility, the readiness to direct behavior toward organizational goals—all are present in people. The administrator does not put them there. It is a responsibility of the administration to make it possible for people to recognize and develop these human characteristics for themselves.
4. The essential task of the administrator is to arrange organizational conditions and methods of operation so that people can achieve their own goals best by directing their own efforts toward organizational objectives.[11]

Much has been written about the concept of the self-fulfilling prophecy: An administrator sets up a system of control, hard or soft, which tends to create the kind of behavior he expects. People then behave in varying ways, largely because such behavior is expected. Organizational behavior, therefore, is believed to be a matter of administrative perception, rather than a result of man's inherent nature.

McGregor's work has been misunderstood by many. There has been a tendency to categorize behaviors as "Theory X behaviors" or "Theory Y behaviors," and this is misleading. X and Y are sets of assumptions about people as they are; they are not intended to describe manifest behavior patterns. There are some who suggest that, any time a principal or an administrator behaves in a direct, controlling fashion, he is a "Theory X" person and that, any time he behaves in a kindly, indirective fashion, he is a "Theory Y" person. Such an oversimplification of the concepts performs but small service. Theory Y simply suggests that man is a learning, growing organism, that he is capable of many creative acts and of complex problem solving. It assumes that leadership ability is widely distributed throughout the population and that it would be ineffective organization indeed not to take advantage of this.[12] Implications for a principal are many.

Theory X basically assumes the need for a vast array of external control mechanisms, while Theory Y assumes much employee self-control and self-direction and implies a participatory management system. In neither instance are the goals of the organization forgotten, but the means of achieving them vary widely. A principal who accepts the assumptions of Theory Y might provide more opportunities for leadership on a particular project or task to emerge from the staff rather than considering himself to be the sole source of initiation. Such a principal would encourage activities designed to enlarge the decision-making authority of individual teachers or groups of teachers, thereby giving them more control over their daily professional life. Clearly, too, performance appraisal of teachers and other employees would result from cooperative target setting, rather than the predetermined expectations of a single administrator. Such procedures require greater faith in one's co-workers.

MOTIVATION, MORALE, AND REWARDS

One of the most incisive ways to examine the behavior of people in an organization was provided by Abraham Maslow.[13] His hierarchy of human needs can readily be applied to the motivation and morale of school employees and to the reward system and administrative style employed by a principal.

Early in the 1940's Maslow advanced a theory of human motivation based on five basic human needs: physiological, safety, social, esteem, and self-actualization. According to the theory, these needs occur in a hierarchy wherein each lower need must be substantially satisfied before a higher one, serving in turn as a mediator, becomes apparent. Figure 5-2 depicts this hierarchy.

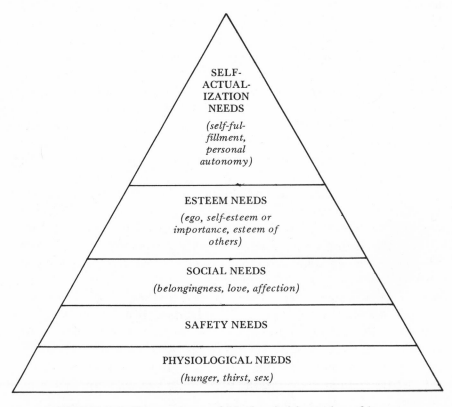

**SELF-
ACTUAL-
IZATION
NEEDS**

*(self-ful-
fillment,
personal
autonomy)*

ESTEEM NEEDS

*(ego, self-esteem or
importance, esteem of
others)*

SOCIAL NEEDS

(belongingness, love, affection)

SAFETY NEEDS

PHYSIOLOGICAL NEEDS

(hunger, thirst, sex)

FIGURE 5-2. Dimensions of Maslow's hierarchy of human
needs theory

A statement from Maslow's original work may serve as the best explanation of the theory:

It is quite true that man lives by bread alone—when there is no bread. But what happens to man's desires when there is plenty of bread, and when his belly is chronically filled? At once other (and "higher") needs emerge, and these rather than physiological hunger, dominate the organisms. And when these in turn are satisfied, new (and still "higher") needs emerge, and so on.

Simmons, in a research work which examined teacher satisfaction and dissatisfaction, has pointed out that:

Although Maslow's theory was not originally formulated with reference to job satisfaction, it nevertheless can be so applied. For example, an employee must have his physiological needs satisfied before he is able to achieve self-esteem or self-actualization needs in the work situation. Consequently, an employer should not be concerned with providing challenging work for employee self-esteem needs if he is not paying his workers enough so that they can eat fairly well, since the employees are primarily motivated by needs lower in the hierarchy. Conversely, pay increases are not likely to increase job satisfaction if employees are already paid well. Rather, challenging work or opportunities for increased status would probably provide more direct need satisfaction.[14]

An important part of the theory is that, as one level of need is substantially satisfied, it ceases to motivate. Providing rewards consistent with one needs level to a staff member who is operating at another needs level is not likely to result in the desired behavior.

Most people function above the level of security and physiological needs, needs that are probably met in most school systems. They are reasonably free from capricious administrative action (security), and, while there may be loud disclaimers, they are paid enough to keep themselves reasonably well fed and clothed (physiological) and to participate in the "good life." It is interesting to note that a principal probably has less control over these lower-level rewards in any case, for the ability to reward people at the physiological and security levels is usually circumscribed by the larger organization in terms of a salary schedule.

A principal may, however, have a greater opportunity to effect rewards at the higher levels, which is probably where most members of his staff are operating. His position in the organization may be critical with respect to providing his staff with opportunities for personal growth, for he might well control rewards at the social and ego needs levels.

ROLES WITHIN THE ORGANIZATION

Presthus[15] looked at complex organizations in a global fashion and divided personnel into three rather loosely defined types: *upward-mobile, indifferent,* and *ambivalent.*

The upward-mobile type is more clearly in tune with the goals, purposes, and directions of the organization. In William H. Whyte's parlance, these are the "organization men," the people who are most congruent with the organization's goals.

The indifferent type has a somewhat different orientation. They are the people who "just work here," and they probably comprise a great portion of the personnel in any organization. Such people are, in effect, selling their time, but they also jealously guard the rest of their time. They need the job, and they may be effective in it, but they are less devoted to the total task of the organization and less concerned about its goals, whatever they may be. They could be viewed perhaps as generally less congruent but not deliberately disruptive unless the organization begins to infringe on their "after work" life or has expectations antithetical to the norms of other groups to which they belong.

The third type, labeled ambivalent, would like to succeed personally, but those who fit in this category are either unwilling to put forth the effort to succeed or unsure how to go about it. Presthus sees this type as tending to be most affected by the goals set in other groups, even when such goals are contrary to or at considerable variance with the organization's goals.

Another useful characteristic developed by Gouldner is based on earlier work by Robert Merton.[16] He distinguishes the latent roles of individuals as being *cosmopolitan* and *local.*

Cosmopolitans are "those low on loyalty to the employing organization, high on commitment to specialized role skills, and likely to use an outer reference group orientation." Locals are "those high on loyalty to the employing organization, low on commitment to specialized role skills, and likely to use an inner reference group orientation." Both categories are further subdivided according to specific types and behavior patterns.

Owens has concluded:

The implications of this kind of analysis of behavioral style are clear. Locals and cosmopolitans view their organizations differently and interpret their relationship to them differently; moreover, their behavior style can be influenced by this differing orientation in both formal and informal relationships. In most public school organizations, locals will tend to exercise greater influence in the organization and will achieve greater acceptance in the social system than cosmopolitans. The local-cosmopolitan orientation of staff members can be a very real source of conflict with regard to such issues as views held by teachers concerning the need for rules, the importance of loyalty to the organization, and the question of professional outer-reference orientation versus the value of local longevity of service.[17]

Simply stated, locals confine their interests to their own community; cosmopolitans relate to the outside world as well as to their community. The influence of the local (and his desired rewards) relies on an elaborate network of personal relationships within the school and the community. The cosmopolitan is likely to perceive his influence as necessarily resting far more on technical competence, relying more on an outer-reference group for his rewards. He gains his respect, or expects to do so, as a result of his particular expertise.

These classifications by Presthus and Gouldner are helpful, but they are too broad to be completely definitive. In any classification there is always the risk of overgeneralization. People do not fit neatly into categories. Among other considerations, racial and ethnic differences often affect behavior patterns and responses to organizational constraints or common reward systems employed by administrators.

INFORMAL GROUPS

Organization members satisfy many of their social and ego needs by interacting with their peers. Such rewards are not primarily under the control of the administrator although he might influence the conditions under which such interactions take place.

Functioning within the formal framework of any organization are many informal groupings of people characterized by a general agreement, not necessarily spoken but tacitly understood, as to certain values and goals. These groups, which meet over a cup of coffee or a cigarette during work and perhaps socialize together after work, tend to see things similarly. It is well to remember that there is not usually just one group; more often there are a number of groups. Leadership is earned through power, personality, or prestige, rather than being ascribed as it is in the formal organization. By their very nature, informal groupings are unstable. There are shifts in leadership as members leave the system or as new leaders emerge, and the administrator must be aware of these changes and their implications.

These loosely organized but often powerful groups of people operate outside of the formal organization and outside of the communications channel of the formal organization. They have their own norms, values, and needs, which may or may not be in agreement with the goals or expectations of the formal organization, and they may modify, or actually inhibit, its goals. Ways must be found to assess the needs of these groups as well as those of the formal organization.

Perhaps one of the most difficult problems an administrator faces as he attempts to make use of the informal leadership in his staff is the fear his co-workers may have of being "co-opted." That is, by responding positively to organizational motivation and exerting leadership in the achievement of organizational goals, the informal leader risks losing his influence in the informal dimension.

Members of school organizations, to complicate things further, are often members of other formal organizations which impinge on the school as well as upon their professional and personal lives. Teachers are members of unions and associations, and other, more general self-help groups such as the NAACP, the National Congress of American Indians, or the Southwest Council of La Raza, for example. Any of these other organizations might oppose certain school system procedures and policies from time to time and demand loyalty on the part of their membership, producing strain and internal conflict.

Also, the higher-level rewards traditionally at the disposal of the principal and the school organization may be entirely circumscribed by other organizations to which the teacher belongs. An office in the local union, or an action committee assignment in the Southwest Council of La Raza, for example, may provide considerable psychological reward to the recipient, well beyond anything his principal or the school system can provide with an assignment to teach third grade in Room 201. One might argue that the more successful principal recognizes this and works to develop a school organization within which teachers might receive some of these same psychological rewards.

The orientation a person brings to his work life does affect his behavior in the organization, his reactions to and interactions with others, and his responsiveness to various reward systems at the disposal of the principal. Zeigler provides much insight when he says:

[it is clearly implicit] ... that it is not merely a person's occupation which colors his attitudes, but rather it is his perceptions of his occupation and the extent to which the occupation is functional in maintaining an integrated personality. On the other hand, there is the question of commitment to the occupation. To some persons the occupation is a major component of their identity. Others look at the occupation in a more casual fashion, viewing it primarily as a money-making device and not so much a portion of a total life-style.[18]

More characteristic of large complex school systems are individual school faculties which more generally reflect our culturally pluralistic society. Many people on a school staff will not derive their normative behavior from a white, middle-class heritage—equally true, of course, of the student body. Responses to traditional control and decision systems in the organization may vary from hostile acquiescence to open challenge, although not always as a result of ethnic, racial, or cultural differences.[19] Knowing a district, much as a salesman knows his territory, is the key.

In a very real sense the official power of the principal is circumscribed from two sources: the superordinate structure with its formal policies and procedures, and the subordinate structure with its unions, associations, and informal power groups.

The principal must accept his co-workers as products of many intrapsychical and extraorganizational forces, not given to responding similarly to the same motivational devices and not equally able to accept or understand the same overt behavior of the principal. This makes the task of developing an effective work group complex indeed. The establishment of workable interpersonal relations depends in great part on the ability of individuals to accept their differing orientations and formulate a high level of mutual trust.

INDIVIDUAL AND GROUP RELATIONS

One of the clearest ways of analyzing the individual in relation to others in the group is through the use of Luft's Johari Awareness Model[20] depicted in Figure 5-3.

This model represents the total person in relation to other persons based on an awareness of behavior, feelings, motivation, and other factors. An act or feeling is assigned to a particular quadrant based on the individual's or others' awareness of it, and the quadrants are defined as:

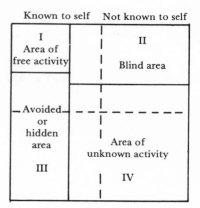

THE QUADRANTS

BEGINNING
INTERACTION IN A NEW GROUP

EXPANDED AREA OF FREE
ACTIVITY (an effective group)

FIGURE 5-3. Johari window

Quadrant 1—the open segment, refers to behavior, feelings, and motivation known to the self and to others;

Quadrant 2—the blind segment, refers to behavior, feelings, and motivation known to others but not to the self;

Quadrant 3—the hidden segment, refers to behavior, feelings, and motivation known to the self but not to others;

Quadrant 4—the unknown segment, refers to behavior, feelings, and motivation known neither to the self nor to others.[21]

The model implies a close relationship between interpersonal relations and group effectiveness. For example, a large open area of free activity indicates mutual trust and respect among the individuals which results in good interaction and effective communication. Thus, initial interaction in a new group should focus on the development of trust and respect among group members.

Luft has said:

Change may mean threat, and it is understandable that people's defenses may be aroused. It is not enough to rework the vocabulary and call for "problem-solving" instead of "change." The most important thing in promoting real change appears to be organizational and interpersonal climate.

Climate is important because the *process* of solving problems is as significant as the solutions. Good ideas alone are not enough. Concern for persons and their feelings is crucial. *Robert's Rules of Order* or parliamentary procedure may seem efficient, but they often create a win-lose situation. Large group meetings require some structure, but no more than is necessary. Usually too much structure is imposed, thereby increasing the chances of proper form at the expense of individual feelings. The subtleties of group processes are active even if never mentioned. Feelings of insecurity seem to permeate most face-to-face interactions in faculty meetings, and these feelings can become transformed into anger and defensiveness rather quickly. It takes time for ruffled feelings to be expressed and for face to be saved. This is the same as saying that it takes time to build a psychological climate for real collaboration. People learn quite soon whether dissent is tolerated; innovation without the feeling that it is all right to dissent is cotton candy.

Interpersonal relationships throughout an organization affect the general psychological climate, and the attitudes of the organization affect interpersonal relations: parts and wholes influence each other.[22]

The Luft model might be used by a school principal interested in developing a more effective faculty group. If the faculty as a group has a very small area of free activity, the group will not be able to deal with significant problems, and communication will remain at a very superficial level. Staff members will tend to say what they think the principal or the group wants them to say, not what they really feel. If blind, hidden, or unknown areas are infringed upon, a group member (or members) will feel threatened and withdraw from active participation in the group. Before a school staff can be an effective group able to solve the problems confronting the school, it must be able to examine, without defensiveness, the various aspects of an issue and deal effectively with conflict.

Schutz[23] has developed a theory of interpersonal relations that identifies three interpersonal need areas: inclusion, or the need to establish and maintain a satisfactory relation with people in terms of association; control, or the need to establish and maintain a satisfactory relation with people in terms of force and power; and affection, or the need to establish and maintain a satisfactory relation with people in terms of caring and love. These three areas can be used to explain and predict interpersonal behavior in terms of expressed behavior (actions taken by a person) and wanted behavior (actions of other people that satisfy one or more of the three interpersonal needs). This theory can be illustrated as:

Dimension	Expressed behavior	Wanted behavior
Inclusion	I initiate interaction with people	I want to be included
Control	I control people	I want people to control me
Affection	I act close and personal toward people	I want people to get close and personal with me

Effective interpersonal relations of two or more people depend upon their ability to satisfy reciprocally each other's interpersonal needs, their complementarity regarding both originating and receiving behavior in each need area, and their similarity with respect to the amount of interchange wanted with others in each need area. Compatibility is based on the relative congruency of expressed and wanted behaviors; conflict or incompatibility results from the incongruency of such behaviors. The value of Schutz's theory is that it can be applied to predicting and analyzing conflict that stems from interpersonal relations, given the orientations of the group members and the interpersonal descriptions of the interaction circumstances.

Conflict is often viewed negatively, as being threatening and detrimental to group effectiveness. It may, however, indicate a healthy group in which individuals feel free to present alternatives and take stands on issues important to them personally. It may also be a way of clarifying values and goals and of providing feedback about personal concerns and feelings. Attempts to suppress conflict can actually hamper group effectiveness.

Effective groups ordinarily do not just "happen." The principal must be aware that a climate of mutual trust and respect is needed in order to develop channels for communication and paths toward interaction. This means that he must recognize the influence of informal groups in the school, be able to deal positively with conflict, utilize appropriate types of decision making, and use his staff effectively to solve problems confronting the school.

COMMUNICATION IN THE SCHOOL SETTING

Luft, among others, has pointed out that the establishment of a workable interpersonal relationship depends on the willingness of individuals to exchange information. When information is exchanged, it can be assumed that there is a commitment to cooperation and to the development of mutual trust on the part of the individuals involved.

Although improved techniques of communication have been a major concern for many centuries, the science of communication, the systematic study of human interaction, is of relatively recent origin. Early theories conceptualized communication as a technical process, which is illustrated in Figure 5-4. Later studies added a more human dimension by including the consideration of group dynamics and individual personality factors. Organizations originally studied how to achieve more effective communications at the formal bureaucratic level. More recently attention has shifted to describing the organization as an ever-changing system of interaction, with communication being vital to the maintenance and growth of the entire organization. Only through effective communication can members of the organization remain aware of its goals, relate their work and the work of others to the goals, and contribute to the improvement of organizational procedures.

Barnlund suggests that the attitudes people have toward each

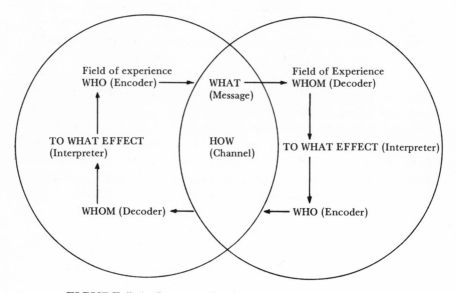

FIGURE 5-4. Communication as a technical process

other, which cause attraction, avoidance, and indifference, are essentially measures of the communication gap between them.[24] To know lines of attraction and avoidance within an organization is to be able to predict where messages will originate, to whom they will flow, and much about how they will be received.

Several studies have focused on organizational elements that facilitate or inhibit communication. Erickson and Pederson[25] reviewed a number of studies having to do with communication within schools, focusing primarily upon such deterrents as the hierarchical structure of the school, the amount of information needing transmission, the lack of collegial interaction, and the factors influencing the interpretation of messages.

A comprehensive survey of inhibitors and facilitators of communication is presented by Havelock in a review of the literature and research about disseminating and utilizing knowledge.[26] Factors that facilitate the communication process are: leadership based on administrative skills such as technical proficiency, organizational ability, and human relations; training programs for both leaders and members emphasizing communication skills; shared perceptions of goals and tasks; participation of peer group members; and overlapping groups in which some individuals have dual memberships.

Theory and research indicate that at least four major elements establish the context of interpersonal communication: verbal communication, nonverbal communication, the environmental setting, and the personalities of the individuals involved. These elements shape interpersonal encounters and influence the interpretation of messages.

Verbal Communication

The concern here is with the words used to express the message. Words, even spoken face to face, do not always convey literal meaning. Verbal communication often becomes the "What did he mean by that?" exchange illustrated by a well-known joke in which two people pass each other on the street. One says, "Good morning"; the other looks puzzled and continues down the street mumbling to himself, "I wonder what he meant by that?"

Hayakawa suggests that one of the basic problems in verbal communication is not in the words themselves but in human reactions to words.[27] When we react to a word, we react to a meaning symbolically attached to it as a result of our past experience. Shared perceptions or mutual understanding is vital for effective verbal communication and emphasizes the need for clarifying verbal messages through skills such as paraphrasing, utilizing appropriate communication channels, and providing for feedback.

Nonverbal Communication

People do not just communicate with each other through written and oral statements. The adage "What you are speaks so loudly that I cannot hear what you say" has been given added meaning as the realm of nonverbal communication has been opened to view. Gesture, tone of voice, posture, or other overt behavior may be as, if not more, important than what is verbally expressed. Mehrabian suggests that the meaning of any message is 7 percent verbal, 38 percent vocal, and 55 percent facial expression and body movement.[28]

Sarcasm, for example, is a message in which the information transmitted vocally contradicts the information transmitted verbally. A smile or frown, a gesture, or a change in body position is a physical communication that may contradict a verbal message.[29] French and

Galloway,[30] among others, have studied problems that arise in the classroom when a teacher's verbal and nonverbal communication is in conflict. Although more research is needed in this area, current studies indicate that, when the verbal, vocal, and physical messages are incongruent, communication problems are likely to occur.

Environmental Setting

The importance of the setting in interpersonal communication is closely related to nonverbal communication. An emerging area of research and study known as environmental design focuses on the psychological effect of such factors as time, space, color, light, noise, and objects on individuals. Edward Hall's writings on the use of space as a factor in communication[31] relate earlier works from psychology and cultural anthropology to modern society and interpersonal relations. The implications of environmental factors for effective communication may be particularly significant for school administrators. Not only what a principal says or does, but also how he arranges the furniture in his office, the time at which he schedules conferences, and the kinds of objects he has on his desk may affect other people's perceptions of him and thus influence the communication process.

Individual Personality Factors

Finally, attitudes and values influence effective communication. For one thing, people tend to prefer communicating with those who reinforce rather than reject their values because contact with such people is more comfortable and satisfying. Another consideration is the degree to which an individual is receptive to new ideas. Many informal communication patterns in the school are a result of personality factors and shared values.

A school principal concerned with improving interpersonal communication must consider his verbal and nonverbal skills, as well as the factors of environment and personality. Communication problems may be related to what Argyris[32] describes as authentic behavior in leadership. Group and individual perceptions of the principal's authenticity may result from congruence among the four elements of interpersonal communication described previously.

THE HUMANE SCHOOL

Individual schools may be described as open living systems stabilized by role expectations and interpersonal norms with predictable behavior evident as a result of shared beliefs about what is appropriate and necessary in the operation of the school. The individual school may also be described as a primary group in which role takers respond to each other with more emotionality and individuality than the more formal bureaucracy.

Increased production or organized goal achievement must include process, as well as ends. Foshay suggests that we must pursue "humane ends in a humane form."[33] If the output of the organization is to be humane, then the participants in that output must be allowed to be humane in this same fashion.

That is, they have to be perceived as people who act as wholes in an endlessly complex fashion. They have to be allowed to behave as individuals if they are to be imaginative and humane themselves.

Perhaps this chapter identifies a new role for the principal: reorganizer of the school environment, a facilitator. This may well describe a person who can take the materiel and the personnel (including students) and put them into a new kind of relationship that will provide for the humane school—the school for human beings—organized with some understanding about the way human beings learn, grow, and develop. It would be a relaxed school in which there would be great concern for the physical, social, psychological, as well as the intellectual, needs of the people who work and learn in that school.

We offend against almost everything we know about people in schools as they are now organized, where everybody has to go to the lavatory at the same time—by the number and in the straight line—and, one might presume, on cue. Where are the music, the art, the bright colors, the relaxed atmosphere that ought to accompany joyful experiences? Learning should indeed be a joyful experience, fraught with discovery and challenge. Is music confined to the music room? Art to the art room? Are teachers' laughs confined to the teachers' lounge? Are bright colors to be found only on the Scott Foresman calendar in sharp contrast to the institutional green of the walls?

The school is often an "uptight" place. The primary role of the principal might well be to understand the nature of freedom and set the tone for it in the school. Such a role calls for great flexibility and great confidence in the abilities of others. It is no longer a question of not accepting this new role; it is being thrust on the principal.

Four forces are at work which demand that the school climate change:

1. *The changing nature of students.* They are more aware, more questioning, more insistent that they be a *part* of the action rather than always being acted upon.

2. *The increased competence, power, and militance of teachers.* Teachers are more conscious of their competence, less drone-like, more questioning, and they, too, insist on being part of the action.

3. *The impact of technology.* Teachers and administrators have been freed from many of the mundane tasks and routine work, allowing them more time to individualize instruction.

4. *Social change, urbanization, and increasing socioeconomic polarization.* New ways of organizing within the school, new ways of behaving, and new reward systems consistent with the cultural pluralism evident in our society are needed, and the varying personal needs of the members of the school organization must also be considered.[34]

These four forces tell the principal that the military-penal model of school organization, with all power and authority issuing from the top, cannot continue. The principal who does not involve his staff and students in participatory decision making and in group goal setting and who does not recognize the need for an open, free climate will not be tolerated for long; his clients, co-workers, and constituents will not permit it. The principal must become an expert on how to change the environment to accomplish the school's goals, rather than being solely a manager or instructional expert.

Kenneth McIntyre of the University of Texas speaks most eloquently about the new principal. One of the qualities most needed, he states, is morality:

When I speak of morality among school principals, I am not suggesting that they are typically subject to unbridled indulgence in carnal passions. In fact, I can't conceive of a less licentious group, outside of a convalescent home for retired fundamentalist ministers. My concern is with the broad issues of rightness and wrongness, with sensitivity to human need and feeling, with compassion for the weak and helpless, with ability to love the unlovely, with passion for freedom with responsibility.

A moral school principal, as I am using the term *moral*, is one who takes seriously the school's accountability for helping individual human beings to realize their potential. He is almost militant in his determination to overcome obstacles to a decent educational program, as stated by Goldhammer and Becker after their study of more than 300 principals representing every state in the Nation: "In schools that were extremely good we inevitably found an aggressive, professionally alert, dynamic principal determined to provide the kind of educational programs he deemed necessary, no matter what." He is a believer in law and order, and he demonstrates his belief by operating the school in a lawful and orderly manner—including observance of laws, court decisions, and ethical principles pertaining to race, religion, and freedom of expression. He is more concerned with the depth of students' understanding than the length of their hair. He is outraged by the erosion of citizens' constitutional rights, and he scrupulously protects the rights of the citizens in the classrooms. He is, in short, a thoroughly *human* being who is dedicated to the proposition that the schools can be significant instrumentalities in the fulfillment of the American dream—a democracy with liberty and justice for all.

I hope that I am not unbearably sentimentalizing this aspect of the principal's personal makeup, but I am convinced that we have neglected the human, the philosophical, the moral dimensions of administration in the past and we cannot afford to continue this neglect. The kinds of problems pressing in on the schools, and likely to increase in the coming years, cry out for empathy, concern, and compassion—not for the dehumanization that threatens to overwhelm us.[35]

APPLICATION

The final part of this chapter contains three kinds of information. There is a brief discussion of available standardized instruments that investigate human relations and morale in an organization, which is followed by some suggestions relative to relevant in-service activities for administrators and teachers. Finally, there has been an attempt to develop some representative behavioral objectives in the area of interpersonal relations that would assist administrators in beginning self-analysis and group analysis and staff development personnel in developing appropriate local assessment inventories.

Available Instrumentation

Many instruments are presently available for use by building administrators, those central office personnel charged with in-service program development, or, in some instances, specially trained personnel to collect and analyze data about the status and nature of the interpersonal dimension of a school's operation. Some are mentioned in other chapters of this volume (see, especially, Chapter Three). The three instruments examined here bear especially on the interpersonal domain, which, to a degree, forms the essential focus of this chapter.

The first instrument, the Personal Orientation Inventory (POI), has the individual as its primary focus. The other two instruments, the Organizational Climate Descriptive Questionnaire (OCDQ) and the Profile of Organizational Characteristics (POC), focus on the perceptions and attitudes of organizational members about the "way things are" in the organization and provide insight into administrative behavior and group development, as well as the nature of decisional processes and organizational maintenance.

Personal Orientation Inventory.[36] The POI was created to provide a comprehensive measure of values and behavior thought to be important in the development of self-actualization. It contains 150 two-choice comparative value and behavior judgments which are scored twice, first for the two-basic scales of personal orientation, that is, inner-directed support and time competence, and second for ten subscales designed to measure a conceptually important element of self-actualization.

When a gross estimate of an individual's level of self-actualization is desired, only the time competence scale and the inner-directed scales should be scored. The time competence scale measures the degree to which the individual is present-oriented. The inner-directed scale measures whether the individual is independent and self-supportive or dependent and seeks the support of others' views. The ten subscales are composed of two scales each for five aspects of behavior: valuing, feeling, self-perception, synergistic awareness, and interpersonal sensitivity. Elements of the inventory are essentially described in Figure 5-5.

The uses of the POI or similar instruments by those charged with in-service programming and staff development of administrators are varied. They could be used as screening mechanisms in considering administrative appointments since they focus on personal attitudes, beliefs, and orientations that affect the interpersonal relations of principal and staff. They could also be used to evaluate a series of planned in-service training activities dealing with the personal dimension of an administrator's behavior if used for pre- and postdata gathering. Growth (or lack of it) can be plotted on the profile. And they can be used to collect status data that might form the basis for in-service programming.

Profile of Organizational Characteristics. This instrument developed by Rensis Likert[37] issues from a theory of administration and supervision based on three principles: supportive relationships; group decision making and group supervision; and high performance goals for individuals, groups, and the organization.

Four different organizational profiles (management systems) may be determined by the instrument. Because of the interdependence of items, a school could probably not be described as possessing characteristics of more than one organizational type. The organizational profiles are composed of individual tendencies and characteristics, each of which is dependent upon the appearance of others of the same or similar kind and intensity.

Management systems (profiles)	
System 1	Exploitive—Authoritarian
System 2	Benevolent—Authoritarian
System 3	Consultative
System 4	Participative

Systems 1 and 2 differ somewhat, but they generally describe an administrative style based on high control mechanisms, Theory X assumptions, distortion of communication channels, and highly delineated and centralized decision making. Administrators in either of the two systems will find subordinates characterized by low group loyalty, less teamwork and cooperation, lower motivational potential, and other nonproductive characteristics.

System 3 describes an organization that might be in transition. It does not maximize student and teacher actualization nor the achievement of school goals, but it does appear to perform adequately in regard to these aspects.

System 4 is characterized by supportive relationships of group members, an administration based on Theory Y assumptions, individual and group self-control, and opportunities for professional self-actualization.

Organizational Climate Descriptive Questionnaire. The research of Halpin and Croft[38] produced an instrument that describes the personality of schools. Eight subtests comprise the instrument; four in the group characteristics dimension (disengagement, hindrance, esprit, intimacy) and four in the leader behavior dimension (aloofness, production emphasis, thrust, consideration). A profile depicting

PROFILE SHEET FOR THE PERSONAL ORIENTATION INVENTORY

NAME _____

AGE _____ SEX _____

OCCUPATION _____

DATE TESTED _____

I T_I - T_C (Time) Ratio:
Self-Actualizing Average: $T_I:T_C = 1:8$
Your Ratio: $T_I:T_C = 1:$

| 1 | 2 | 3 | 4 | 5 | 6 | 7 | 8 | 9 | 10 |

II O-I (Support) Ratio:
Self-Actualizing Average: $O:I = 1:3$
Your Ratio: $O:I = 1:$

| 1 | 2 | 3 | 4 | 5 | 6 | 7 | 8 | 9 | 10 |

		VALUING		FEELING		SELF-PERCEPTION		SYNERGISTIC AWARENESS		INTERPERSONAL SENSITIVITY	
TIME COMPETENT Lives in the present	INNER-DIRECTED Independent, self-supportive	SELF-ACTUALIZING VALUE Holds values of self-actualizing people	EXISTENTIALITY Flexible in application of values	FEELING REACTIVITY Sensitive to own needs and feelings	SPONTANEITY Freely expresses feelings behaviorally	SELF-REGARD Has high self worth	SELF-ACCEPTANCE Accepting of self in spite of weaknesses	NATURE OF MAN, CONSTRUCTIVE Sees man as essentially good	SYNERGY Sees opposites of life as meaningfully related	ACCEPTANCE OF AGGRESSION Accepts feelings of anger or aggression	CAPACITY FOR INTIMATE CONTACT Has warm interpersonal relationships
T_C	I	SAV	Ex	Fr	S	Sr	Sa	Nc	Sy	A	C

ADULT NORMS

80

— 125
— 120
— 115
— 110 — 25 — 30 — 25
— 105

— 25
— 20 — 20 — 15 — 15 — 15 — 9 — 25
— 20

70

60

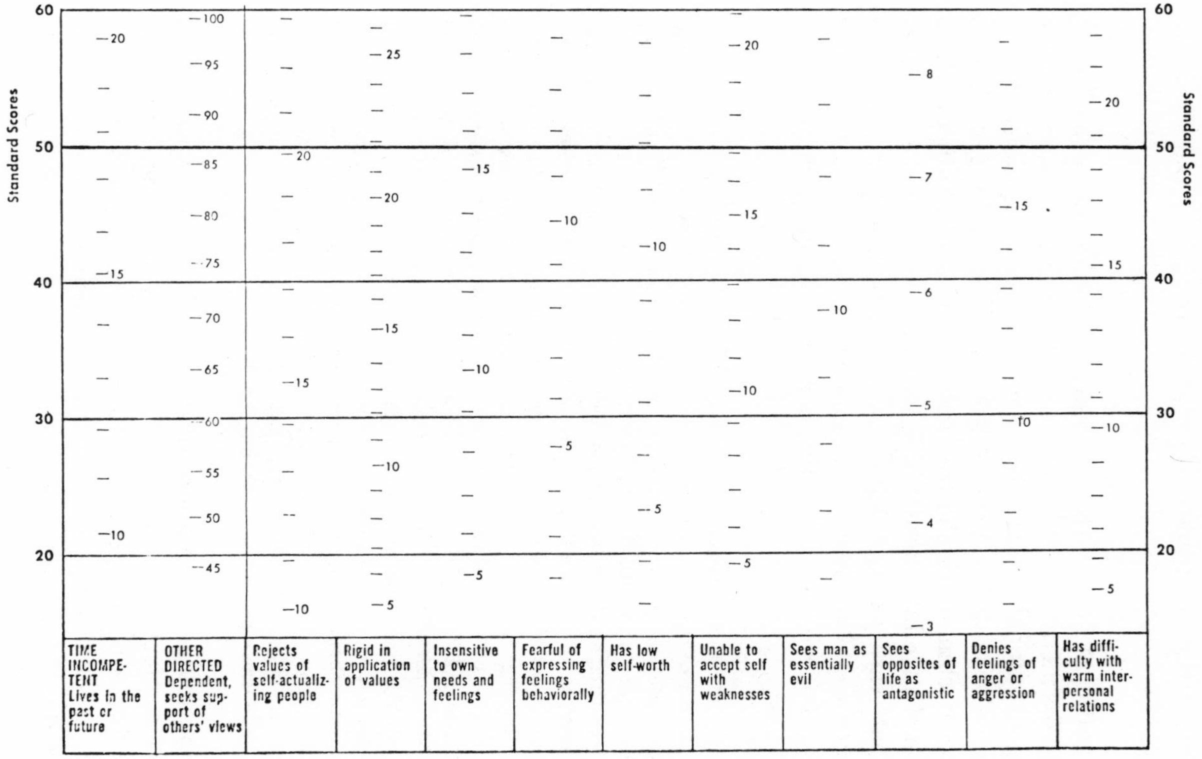

Standard Scores

60   50   40   30   20

| TIME INCOMPE-TENT Lives in the past or future | OTHER DIRECTED Dependent, seeks support of others' views | Rejects values of self-actualiz-ing people | Rigid in application of values | Insensitive to own needs and feelings | Fearful of expressing feelings behaviorally | Has low self-worth | Unable to accept self with weaknesses | Sees man as essentially evil | Sees opposites of life as antagonistic | Denies feelings of anger or aggression | Has diffi-culty with warm inter-personal relations |

FIGURE 5-5. Profile sheet for the personal orientation inventory

the organizational climate can be constructed from the scores of the eight subtests. The six profiles developed by Halpin and Croft are termed: open, autonomous, controlled, familiar, paternal, and closed.

Halpin and Croft found that a school possessing an open climate, which they deemed most effective, was a lively organization, moving toward organizational goals while at the same time providing satisfaction to members of the organization. The operational definition given to open climate emphasizes that this is a situation in which organizational members derive high levels of satisfaction both from interpersonal relations with fellow workers and from accomplishing tasks assigned to them within the organization.

Halpin and Croft described the behavior of the principal of an open school as:

an appropriate integration between his own personality and the role he is required to play as principal. In this respect his behavior can be viewed as "genuine." Not only does he set an example by working hard himself (high *Thrust*) but, depending upon the situation, he can either criticize the actions of teachers or can, on the other hand, go out of his way to help a teacher (high *Consideration*). He possesses the personal flexibility to be "genuine" whether he be required to control and direct the activities of others or be required to show compassion in satisfying the social needs of individual teachers. He has integrity in that he is "all of a piece" and therefore can function well in either situation. He is not *aloof*, nor are the rules and procedures which he sets up inflexible and impersonal. Nonetheless, rules and regulations are adhered to, and through them, he provides subtle direction and control for the teachers. He does not have to *emphasize production*; nor does he need to monitor the teachers' activities closely, because the teachers do, indeed, produce easily and freely. Nor does he do all the work himself; he has the ability to let appropriate leadership acts emerge from the teachers (low *Production Emphasis*). Withal, he is in full control of the situation and he clearly provides leadership for the staff.[39]

One of the guiding assumptions of the work by Halpin and Croft is that the most effective organizational climate will be one in which it is possible for acts of leadership to emerge easily from whatever source. An essential determinant of a school's effectiveness noted by Halpin and Croft[40] was the ascribed leader's ability, or his lack of ability, to create a climate in which he and the other group members could initiate and consummate acts of leadership.

Suggested In-service Programming Activities

Widely varied activities, workshops, and materials that focus on the development of appropriate interpersonal skills for administrators exist. Simulation workshops, and human relations-organizational development laboratories continue to offer much promise. Where these are conducted by qualified personnel, operating from a data base and within a structure of clearly developed objectives, one might expect a high degree of skill development by participants. Reinforcement of such learnings through clinical supervisory activities conducted by those charged with staff development and through in-service workshops on a planned and continuous basis is, of course, most important.

Simulation workshops. Simulation materials are useful as exercises in school group decision making and problem solving. These are normally based on situations and events that are readily localized, yet they have the advantage, by definition, of being "depersonalized." Simulation games provide wide opportunities for self-analysis and group analysis as well as providing a "safe" means of examining consensus decision making and group planning procedures. Exercises in leadership skills identification and development by participants can also be provided, and school staff can be aided in developing the process skills necessary for group problem solving.

Two prime sources for well-developed simulation packages are the University Council for Educational Administration and the Anti-Defamation League of B'nai B'rith. UCEA has produced the Monroe City/URB/SIM materials which focus on school problems in urban areas. Though they have been designed primarily for pre- and in-service use with school administrators, I have used them most successfully with entire school staffs, including teachers, special personnel, and principals. Used in this way, they become a vehicle for testing perceptions, group processes, and the cooperative development of proposed solutions to problems of curriculum planning and race relations.[41]

The Anti-Defamation League's set of simulations materials are directed toward problems of education in a biracial and multicultural setting. Included in the sets are student-teacher-administrator problems, teacher-administrator problems, and teacher-teacher problems.[42] The focus of the materials is interpersonal relations, more especially as these are concerned with social integration in the deseg-regated school.

Human Relations-Organizational Development Workshops. Vari-ous activities and approaches fall under the rubric "human relations workshops." The underlying objective of human relations training is to help individuals understand their own behavior and the behavior of others in a group setting. The sociology and the psychology of groups is the focus.

One might identify two general types of human relations pro-grams, according to whether the emphasis is to be personal growth of the individual or whether it is to be effective group problem solving. Most human relations authorities suggest that the individual be sent to a lab away from home for that personal growth experience. It is important to clearly establish the purpose and objectives of the workshop. The nature and kind of exercises and processes differ considerably according to the purpose intended. Birnbaum's "Sense about Sensitivity Training" should be required reading for anyone considering the use of human relations workshops in school sys-tems.[43] Birnbaum states that, "when lab organizers are unable or unwilling to differentiate between various kinds of training, the re-sults can be disastrous."[44]

Essentially, training activities which focus on organizational change, problems of morale, and human relations in an organization provide good substance for in-district workshops.[45] The emphasis is on increasing the effectiveness of the individual in the organization. Where the focus is to be primarily on personal growth, the recom-mendation is that lab participation be in a setting away from home where there can be relative anonymity for the individual.[46]

Self-analysis and Group Analysis: Checking Perceptions

This chapter has been concerned with the principal's role in devel-oping effective human relations and morale in the school organiza-tion. The domain can be treated as discrete, of course, only for purposes of presentation and discussion; it is pervasive, impinging on all of the other domains discussed in this volume.

There are two focuses. One focus concerns individual characteris-tics of the principal as he goes about relating to other members of the school organization, and it deals with interpersonal skills such as trustful behavior, authenticity, support for staff, empathy, and communication skills. The other focus concerns behavior of the principal as he attempts to facilitate good relations between and among others. It involves, for example, ways of organizing personnel to accomplish tasks, conflict management techniques, and facilitation of inter- and intragroup communication.

The three standardized instruments discussed earlier provide useful data about perceived principal behavior with respect to both of these focuses, and they reflect the theory base presented in this chapter. The two types of in-service education programs for administrators and teachers—simulation workshops and organizational development workshops—discussed in the context of this chapter have also shown much promise.

A DEVELOPING LIST OF PERFORMANCE CRITERIA

Several important elements of organizational life have implications for the development of a productive work climate. The following list of performance criteria represents elements of organizational life which affect the nature of human relations and morale. For clarification, as well as for reader convenience, the corresponding heading from the text of the chapter is given for each of the concepts identified below. Following each concept statement, specific performance statements relate to fostering effective human relations and morale, and the performance statements are further defined by several indicators of attainment. (The listing of the performance statements and the indicators is not exhaustive; an interesting and perhaps fruitful exercise for the reader would be to extend the list of both, making direct application to a known local setting.)

CONCEPT 1

The school organization is multifunctional and some of the functions are a product of the personal needs and wants of individual organizational members. (See "The Multifunctional Organization" in text.)

Performance Statement

The principal recognizes that the private goals of organizational members affect the achievement of the public goals of the school.

Indicators

1. Recognizes and supports differing teaching styles
2. Flexibly schedules institutional demands on employee time

3. Is able to identify personal needs of individual colleagues and provides intra-organizational ways in which these needs may be satisfied consistent with organizational goals
4. Matches teaching skills with teaching arrangement

Performance Statement

The principal recognizes that individual staff members may have differing value orientations and respond differently to various elements (formal constraints, reward systems, motivators, etc.) of organizational life.

Indicators

1. Can identify and describe unique competencies of staff members
2. Overtly (behaviorally) supports individual staff members' need for personal development and pride in cultural or ethnic background
3. Reveals respect for differing life styles by responding to these in a nonjudgmental way

CONCEPT 2

Creativity and decision-making ability are widely distributed in the population and are not determined by the formal office a person holds. It is possible to provide for the effective use of these abilities within the formal organization. (See "Assumptions about People" and "Motivation, Morale, and Rewards" in text.)

Performance Statement

The principal establishes broad parameters, consistent with general school policies and good educational practice, within which individual staff members or identified groups of staff members have wide latitude for problem resolution and final decision making.

Indicators

1. There arc in evidence "task force teams" of staff members with evident refined responsibilities focusing on significant aspects of the school operation
2. There are well-understood processes or procedures for identifying potential school problems, or curricular instructional needs. Individual staff members know these processes and procedures and invoke them at appropriate times
3. The decision-making process is varied according to the nature of the decision situation (i.e., unilateral decisions in "crisis" situations are made without apology or need for apology; there are in evidence, however, "sensing" mechanisms [Indicator No. 2, above] whereby many crises are anticipated)

Performance Statement

The principal is "authentic" in his dealings with staff members.

Indicators

1. His behavior is perceived by co-workers as congruent with the organizational tasks to be performed (i.e., the staff feels certain jobs and tasks accrue to the "principalship," and it is their belief that their principal is performing these)

2. His behaviors are perceived by others in a manner consistent with the principal's perceptions of his own behavior
3. The principal *violates* unreasonable or inappropriate system-wide policies in favor of his staff

Performance Statement

The principal varies the reward systems at his disposal consistent with the needs of individual staff members and with cognizance that most staff members are probably operating on needs levels above "physiological and security." (This latter should be checked in individual school settings, and, if it is not so, appropriate administrative efforts should be directed toward corrective action.)

Indicators

1. There is in existence a regular formal mechanism (e.g., newsletters) whereby the principal and other staff members announce "jobs well done" by others or where an individual can submit his own announcements of recent professional or personal activities in which he has been engaged
2. There are in evidence "task groups" within which leadership is "achieved," i.e., it devolves to the leader from his peers. Once achieved, such leadership is acknowledged by the principal, publicly and privately
3. There is in evidence flexible scheduling of staff time in order that meetings of appropriate groups may occur within the normal school day or that individual teachers may be released from normal duties for periods of time to conduct research, update skills, serve on system-wide committees, or attend to certain personal activities, etc.
4. Evidences and uses staff evaluation procedures or instruments which focus on the teaching act and subsequent learner achievement of, or movement toward, mutually agreed-upon goals, rather than focusing on extraneous, unnegotiated, or unstated factors

CONCEPT 3

There are two dimensions in complex organizations: formal and informal. The informal dimension has great influence upon individual behavior, provides its own system of rewards, and may or may not exhibit goals congruent with the formal organization. (See "Roles within the Organization," "Informal Groups," and "Individual and Group Relations" in text.)

Performance Statement

The principal is aware of informal groups within the school.

Indicators

1. He is able to identify the informal social or professional groupings in his school and can identify the achieved leaders of these groups
2. There are frequent meetings, informal and formal, with informal staff leaders to discuss matters of significance to the formal dimension of the school organization

Performance Statement

The principal is concerned with the individual staff members' sense of belonging and security within faculty groups.

Indicators

1. Attitude toward individuals who may not conform to normative organizational standards (e.g., dress) is positive and supportive
2. He utilizes various mechanisms such as informal teas or cocktail parties and "buddy systems" to assist in the orientation of new members. Such mechanisms are utilized throughout the year

Performance Statement

The principal develops congruence between individual needs and organizational role expectations.

Indicators

1. Job descriptions or responsibilities of the staff are generally developed in a behaviorist manner rather than in an integrationist manner (A behaviorist model assumes that individuals have as much impact on organization as the reverse; thus, the functions of a particular job are modified to fit the competencies which the job incumbent has. An integrationist model on the other hand defines the job and attempts to fit the individual to it.)
2. Individual staff members are required to generate specific "Job Targets" on an annual basis, and these are negotiated and agreed upon by the principal and the staff member early in the school year (Process as well as product targets are employed.)

CONCEPT 4

Effective organizations are characterized by a variety of communications media and a free flow of information laterally and vertically throughout the organization. Individual units of the organization (schools) place a somewhat heavy reliance on face-to-face communication wherein such elements as nonverbal cues, environmental setting, and individual personality variables affect the perceived meaning of the messages. (See "Communication in the School Setting" in text.)

Performance Statement

The principal effectively communicates with the staff.

Indicators

1. The medium varies according to the complexity of the message being communicated and the degree of behavior change required by the receivers
2. The medium varies according to the nature of the individual(s) and the number of individuals involved
3. There are provisions for "feedback" (advisory councils, face-to-face question-

ing, etc.) so that understanding of verbal and written messages can be checked with some immediacy

4. There is an awareness of the relationship between environmental setting and effective communication (The objects in the school—accessibility of teacher lounge, principal's office, furniture arrangements, classroom arrangement—are arranged to facilitate communication.)

Performance Statement

The principal facilitates intrastaff professional communication.

Indicator

1. Task force committees (curricular or instructional study groups, etc.) which are formed reflect a "Likert Linking Pin" structure (i.e., official professional groupings reflect cross-departmental, cross-grade levels)

CONCLUSION

The preceding list of concepts, performance statements, and indicators of performance levels should provide a good basis either for self-analysis of principal behavior in the human relations and morale domain or for data collection through structured interviews and "on site" observations by an independent reviewer or review team. The effort has been to develop precise "indicators" which could be readily verified. I am aware that I did not wholly succeed in this effort, but I hope that sufficient specificity and substance exist so that users will be able to provide a better evaluation of administrative performance.

NOTES

1. In a "primary group," role takers respond to each other with more emotionality and individuality as compared to the more formal bureaucracy.

2. Solomon E. Asch, *Social Psychology* (New York: Prentice-Hall, 1952).

3. Amitai Etzioni, "Two Approaches to Organizational Analysis: A Critique and a Suggestion," *Administrative Science Quarterly*, 5 (September 1960), pp. 257-78.

4. Jacob W. Getzels, "Administration as a Social Process," in A. W. Halpin (ed.), *Administrative Theory in Education* (Chicago: Midwest Administration Center, University of Chicago), pp. 151-59.

5. A good explanation of the social systems model can be found in Roald T. Campbell *et al.*, *Introduction to Educational Administration* (Boston: Allyn and Bacon, Inc., 1971), ch. 8.

6. In what has become a classic piece of literature about organizations,

Barnard advanced the concept that organizations must be concerned with both effectiveness and efficiency. To Barnard, effectiveness meant the achievement of the goals of the institution, while efficiency reflected achievement with appropriate regard for the people in the organization. (Chester J. Barnard, *The Functions of the Executive* [Cambridge, Mass.: Harvard University Press, 1938].)

7. Jacob W. Getzels and Egon Guba, "Social Behavior and the Administrative Process," *The School Review*, 65 (Winter 1957), pp. 423-41. See also, Roald Campbell, "Implications for the Practice of Administration"; Daniel E. Griffiths, "The Nature and Meaning of Theory," in *Behavioral Science and Educational Administration*, 63rd Yearbook of the National Society for the Study of Education (Chicago: University of Chicago Press, 1964).

8. No implicit criticism is intended of Carnegie or others who have developed human relations training packages. The rationale upon which the Carnegie approach is based, for example, is that one meets his own needs only as he helps others meet their needs. There can be little disagreement with this concept. Often, however, in the aftermath of training programs the concept has been observed to be forgotten, and the efforts of trainees have been directed more toward the accomplishment of certain external mannerisms.

9. See Chris Argyris, *Interpersonal Competence in Organizational Effectiveness* (Homewood, Ill.: The Dorsey Press, Inc., 1962), for a more complete explanation of this concept.

10. Douglas M. McGregor, *The Human Side of the Enterprise* (New York: McGraw-Hill, 1960).

11. The two sets of assumptions are adapted from Douglas M. McGregor, "The Human Side of the Enterprise," in Warren G. Bennis, Kenneth D. Benne, and Robert Chin (eds.), *The Planning of Change* (New York: Holt, Rinehart and Winston, 1962). See also McGregor, *Human Side of the Enterprise* and *The Professional Manager* (New York: McGraw-Hill, 1967).

12. John J. Morse and Jay W. Lorsch present an interesting extension and modification of McGregor's concepts in "Beyond Theory Y," *Harvard Business Review* (May-June 1970), pp. 61-68.

13. A. H. Maslow, *Motivation and Personality* (New York: Harper and Brothers, 1954), and "A Theory of Motivation," *Psychology Review*, 50 (July 1943), 370-96.

14. Robert M. Simmons, "The Measurement of Factors of Teacher Satisfaction and Dissatisfaction in Teaching," doctoral dissertation, University of Tennessee, 1970, p. 24.

15. Robert Presthus, *The Organizational Society* (New York: Vintage Books, 1962).

16. Alvin W. Gouldner, "Cosmopolitans and Locals: Toward an Analysis of Latent Social Roles," *Administrative Science Quarterly*, 11 (December 1957, March 1958); Robert Merton, *Social Theory and Social Structure* (Glencoe, Ill.: Free Press, 1957).

17. Robert Owens, *Organizational Behavior in Schools* (Englewood Cliffs, N.J.: Prentice-Hall, 1970).

18. Harmon Zeigler, *The Political World of the High School Teacher* (Eugene, Ore.: Center for the Advanced Study of Educational Administration, University of Oregon, 1966).

19. An interesting and informative adventure for a white administrator might be to read William H. Grier and Price M. Cobbs's *Black Rage* (New York: Basic Books, 1968) for insights into some of the intrapsychical forces at work on many blacks. A further source of a more general nature may be found in the multiethnic simulation materials published by the Anti-Defamation League. (See, especially, Frederick P. Venditti, *Solving Multi-Ethnic Problems: A Guide Book for Leaders of Small Group Discussions* (New York: Anti-Defamation League of B'nai B'rith, 1970).)

20. Joseph Luft, *Group Processes*, 2nd edition (Palo Alto, Calif.: National Press Books, 1970).

21. *Ibid.*, p. 12.

22. *Ibid.*, p. 65.

23. William C. Schutz, *Leaders of Schools* (Washington, D. C.: U.S. Department of Health, Education, and Welfare, Office of Education, 1966), ch. 4, p. 4.

24. Dean C. Barnlund, *Interpersonal Communication: Survey and Studies* (Boston: Houghton Mifflin Co., 1968), p. 4.

25. Donald A. Erickson and George K. Pederson, "Major Communication Problems in the Schools," *Administrators Notebook* (March 1966), pp. 1-4.

26. Ronald G. Havelock, *Planning for Innovation through Dissemination and Utilization of Knowledge* (Ann Arbor: Institute for Social Research, University of Michigan, 1969), pp. 6-27 to 6-37.

27. S. I. Hayakawa, *Symbol, Status, and Personality* (New York: Harcourt, Brace and World, Inc., 1958), p. 6.

28. Albert Mehrabian, "Communication without Words," *Psychology Today*, 2 (No. 4, Sept. 1968), pp. 52-55.

29. Reynolds found that a principal's nonverbal behavior influences teachers' positive or negative perceptions about a teacher-principal conference. (John Reynolds, "A Study of Nonverbal Communications as Related to Three Educational Administration Situations," doctoral dissertation, University of Tennessee, 1971.)

30. Russell French and Charles M. Galloway, "Communication Events: A New Look at Classroom Interactions," *Educational Leadership*, 27 (No. 6, March 1970), pp. 548-52.

31. Edward T. Hall, *The Hidden Dimension* (New York: Doubleday and Company, Inc., 1969).

32. Argyris, *Interpersonal Competence*.

33. Arthur W. Foshay, "Curriculum Development and the Humane Qualities," in *To Nurture Humaneness*, 1970 Yearbook, Association for Supervision and Curriculum Development (Washington, D. C.: the Association, pp. 143-53.

34. A primary source for these ideas is K. E. McIntyre (ed.), *The Principalship in the 1970's* (Austin: Bureau of Laboratory Schools, University of Texas, 1971), pp. 87-88.

35. *Ibid.*

36. Further information about the POI is available from Educational and Industrial Testing Service, San Diego, California, 92107. It can be scored either by hand or by machine.

37. Rensis Likert, *The Human Organization: Its Management and Value* (New York: McGraw-Hill, 1967 [Appendix II contains the instrument]). Much of the theoretical framework for the instrument was developed in Likert's *New Patterns of Management* (New York: McGraw-Hill, 1961).

38. Andrew W. Halpin and Don B. Croft, *The Organizational Climate of Schools* (Chicago: University of Chicago, Midwest Administration Center, 1963). (The instrument itself is now copyrighted; published and distributed by Macmillan.)

39. *Ibid.*, pp. 61-62.

40. *Ibid.*

41. See Gerald R. Rasmussen and Larry W. Hughes, "Simulation: It's the Real Thing," *NASSP Bulletin*, 11 (March 1972), pp. 76-81. See also Thomas F. Koerner (ed.), *Where Will They Find It? Pre-service and Continuing Education: The Principal's Search* (Washington, D. C.: National Association of Secondary School Principals, 1972).

42. These materials were developed for B'nai B'rith by Frederick P. Venditti, Director of Educational Opportunities Planning Center at the University of Tennessee.

43. Max Birnbaum, "Sense about Sensitivity Training," *Saturday Review* (November 15, 1969), pp. 82-83+. Birnbaum is Director of the Boston University Human Relations Laboratory.

44. *Ibid.*, p. 96.

45. The Center for the Advanced Study of Educational Administration (CASEA) at the University of Oregon has several good publications and studies available about organizational development workshops. See Richard A. Schmuck, Philip J. Runkel, and Daniel Langmeyer, *Theory to Guide Organizational Training in Schools* (Eugene, Ore.: CASEA, 1969), for an example of this effort.

46. A good source for those interested in understanding more about human relations laboratory sessions, especially T-grouping and the diagnosis of group behavior, is the revised NFL Institute for Applied Behavioral Sciences publication, *Reading Book: Laboratories in Human Relations Training*, published by the National Education Association in 1969. The publication is mostly a series of informal papers which deal with important concepts and ideas useful for laboratory sessions. Critical to good human relations laboratories and organizational development labs is a competent, experienced director.

SELECTED REFERENCES

Asch, Solomon E. *Social Psychology*. New York: Prentice-Hall, 1952.

Barnlund, Dean C. *Interpersonal Communication: Survey and Studies*. Boston: Houghton Mifflin Co., 1968.

Bennis, Warren G., Edgar H. Schein, David Berlew, and Fred Steele. *Interpersonal Dynamics: Essays and Readings in Human Interaction.* Homewood, Illinois: Dorsey Press, 1964.

Coleman, James S. *The Adolescent Society.* New York: Free Press, 1961.

Culbertson, Jack A., Paul B. Jacobson, and Theodore L. Reller. *Administrative Relationships: A Casebook.* Englewood Cliffs, New Jersey: Prentice-Hall, Inc., 1960.

Erickson, Donald A., and George K. Pederson. "Major Communication Problems in the Schools." *Administrators Notebook*, March 1966.

Foshay, Arthur W. "Curriculum Development and the Humane Qualities." In *To Nurture Humaneness*, Yearbook, Association for Supervision and Curriculum Development, 1970, pp. 143-153.

French, Russell, and Charles M. Galloway. "Communication Events: A New Look at Classroom Interactions." *Educational Leadership*, Vol. 27, No. 6, March 1970.

Goldman, Samuel. *The School Principal.* New York: The Center for Applied Research in Education, Inc., 1966.

Gouldner, Alvin W. "Cosmopolitans and Locals: Toward an Analysis of Latent Social Roles." *Administrative Science Quarterly*, Vol. 2, December 1957, March 1958.

_____. "Theoretical Requirements of the Applied Social Sciences." *American Sociological Review*, Vol. 22, 1957.

Grier, William H., and Price M. Cobbs. *Black Rage.* New York: Basic Books, 1968.

Griffiths, Daniel E. "The Nature and Meaning of Theory." In *id.* (ed.), *Behavioral Science and Educational Administration, 63rd Yearbook*, National Society for the Study of Education, Chicago: University of Chicago Press, 1964.

_____. *Human Relations in School Administration.* New York: Appleton-Century-Crofts, Inc., 1956.

Hall, Edward T. *The Hidden Dimension.* Garden City, New York: Doubleday and Co. Inc., 1966.

_____. *The Silent Language.* Garden City, New York: Doubleday and Co. Inc., 1959.

Havelock, Ronald G. *Planning for Innovation through Dissemination and Utilization of Knowledge.* Ann Arbor: Institute for Social Research, University of Michigan, 1969.

Hayakawa, S. I. *Symbol, Status, and Personality.* New York: Harcourt, Brace and World, Inc., 1958.

Koerner, Thomas F. (ed.). *Where Will They Find It? Pre-Service and Continuing Education: The Principal's Search.* Washington, D.C.: National Association of Secondary School Principals, 1972.

Likert, Rensis. *The Human Organization: Its Management and Value.* New York: McGraw-Hill, 1967.

Luft, Joseph. *Group Processes,* 2nd edition. Palo Alto, California: National Press Books, 1970.

McIntyre, K. E. (ed.). *The Principalship in the 1970's.* Austin: Bureau of Laboratory Schools, University of Texas, 1971.

Maslow, A. H. *Motivation and Personality.* New York: Harper and Bros., 1954.

————. "A Theory of Motivation." *Psychology Review,* Vol. 50, July 1943.

Mehrabian, Albert. "Communication without Words." *Psychology Today,* Vol. 2, No. 4, September 1968.

Merton, Robert. *Social Theory and Social Structure.* Glencoe, Illinois: Free Press, 1957.

Miles, Raymond E. "Human Relations or Human Resources?" *Harvard Business Review,* Vol. 43, No. 4, July-August 1965.

Owens, Robert. *Organizational Behavior in Schools.* Englewood Cliffs, New Jersey: Prentice-Hall, 1970.

Presthus, Robert. *The Organizational Society.* New York: Vintage Books, 1962.

Rasmussen, Gerald R., and Larry W. Hughes. "Simulation: It's the Real Thing." *NASSP Bulletin,* March 1972.

Reynolds, John. "A Study of Nonverbal Communications as Related to Three Educational Administration Situations." Doctoral dissertation, University of Tennessee, 1971.

Schmuck, Richard A. *Organizational Training for a School Faculty.* Eugene, Oregon: Center for the Advanced Study of Educational Administration, 1970.

————, Philip J. Runkel, and Daniel Langmeyer. *Theory to Guide Organizational Training in Schools.* Eugene, Oregon: Center for the Advanced Study of Educational Administration, 1969.

————, and Matthew B. Miles (eds.). *Organizational Development in Schools.* Palo Alto, California: National Press Books, 1971.

Schutz, William C. *Leaders of Schools.* Washington, D. C.: U.S. Department of Health, Education, and Welfare, Office of Education, 1966.

Sergiovanni, Thomas J., and Robert J. Starratt. *Emerging Patterns of Supervision: Human Perspectives.* New York: McGraw-Hill, 1971.

Simmons, Robert M. "The Measurement of Factors of Teacher Satisfaction and Dissatisfaction in Teaching." Doctoral dissertation, University of Tennessee, 1970.

Trusty, Francis M. *Administering Human Resources.* Berkeley, California: McCutchan Publishing Corporation, 1971.

Venditti, Frederick P. *Solving Multi-Ethnic Problems: A Guidebook for Leaders of Small Group Discussions.* New York: Anti-Defamation League of B'nai B'rith, 1970.

Weart, David N. "The Relationship between Interpersonal Orientations of Teachers and Principals and Satisfaction with Conflict Management Techniques." Doctoral dissertation, University of Rochester, 1972.

Zeigler, Harmon. *The Political World of the High School Teacher.* Eugene, Oregon: Center for the Advanced Study of Educational Administration, 1966.

SIX

ADMINISTERING AND IMPROVING THE INSTRUCTIONAL PROGRAM

Kenneth E. McIntyre

Instruction is a central subsystem of the total educational system, and administering and improving the instructional program is an important domain of responsibility for school principals. Although these assumptions are occasionally disputed, the arguments usually involve the setting up of a straw man (the principal can't be expected to be an expert supervisor and spend half of his time sitting in the back of classrooms), only to be followed by the demolition of said straw man (the principal's role and that of the instructional supervisor differ greatly, and both roles are important).

To contend that administering and improving the instructional program is of prime importance is not to argue that principals in general are conspicuously effective in this aspect of the position, nor to hold that teachers typically see their principals as valuable sources of supervisory assistance. The studies are all too clear on this point.[1] And, whatever shortcomings there have been in the performance of principals, and in their preparation programs and in-service training,

In preparing this chapter I had the assistance of several colleagues at the University of Texas, Austin. I am particularly indebted to Professor Ben M. Harris, whose insights were substantial and invaluable.

one need not accept the status quo as immutable. Presumably teachers would be more receptive to principals' instructional improvement role if the principals were more competent, which does seem to be the case in those relatively few instances when principals are perceived to be especially helpful. There can be no doubt that superintendents, and principals themselves, are convinced that principals *should* be "instructional leaders"—whatever that term means.

The primary purpose of this chapter is to help school principals develop competency in the administration and improvement of the instructional program in their school units. By setting forth the competencies that appear to be required for effective performance and by citing some illustrative examples of behavior indicative of such performance, I hope to provide guidelines for skill development; such guidelines could also improve preparation programs if universities tested their offerings and products against them.

CHARACTERISTICS OF PERFORMANCE EVALUATION

Certain characteristics should be present in any sound procedure for evaluating the performance of school principals, in the instruction domain as well as in others. These characteristics are briefly described here:

1. School principals should participate in setting up an evaluation system and in operating it once it has been established. This means that principals should have something to say about the goals of the program and the criteria by which their performance is to be evaluated. Once the system is operational, each principal should participate in the process of stating his performance objectives, determining how progress toward meeting those objectives is to be measured, analyzing and interpreting data, applying findings in order to correct deficiencies, and planning next steps. In this way both the needs of the individual and the needs of the organization can be served, which is seldom the case with traditional evaluation systems.

2. No system for evaluating the performance of school principals (or anyone else) is any stronger than the information base that supports it. Unsupported judgments, the core of most personnel evaluation efforts in schools up to the present time, are of little or no value to the person being evaluated or to the organization in which he works. One essential requirement of an effective system, then, is that

relevant behaviors be amply described in meaningful categories before judging performance.

3. An effective evaluation system should concentrate on relatively
few important categories of performance, rather than dissipating
time and energy on an unmanageable number of meaningless judgments. Goals at every operational level of the organization should be
clearly set forth and articulated, and expectations common to all incumbents in a given position category should be clearly stated. Although many different competencies are required in any school principalship, only a small number are crucial to all principalships, even
those of a given type or level, in a single school district at any given
time. It is these few crucial competencies that should be investigated,
along with one or more that are specific to the individual, the time,
or the situation.

4. Any system for evaluating school principals' work should serve
two major purposes: it should support certain types of administrative
decisions, such as re-employment, reassignment, promotion, or dismissal, and it should improve the principals' performances. Some devices, such as self-ratings, are helpful for the individual but not for
administrative decision making. Much of the generated data can serve
both purposes, but substantially different procedures should be followed in using the data.

5. Any respectable evaluation system requires resources and capa-
bilities that are not presently available in most school districts. At
least one knowledgeable, skilled person must provide leadership, assist in the development of school district and school unit goals, and
assist principals in developing goal-related objectives, measuring progress toward meeting those objectives, and deciding how to use information for improvement purposes. Few school districts have trained
personnel on hand to meet this need, and funds must be made available to find and train the necessary personnel.

With these general guidelines in mind, I have specific suggestions
for evaluating the performance of school principals in administering
and improving the instructional program (see Appendix A). The
terms *administering* and *improving* are used deliberately, to emphasize that maintenance and change are both necessary functions in an
instructional program. Much of a principal's time will of necessity be
spent in certain task areas turning out the products of instruction—
providing staff, space, materials, and the like—so that teaching can be

done with a minimum of confusion. Teachers value this kind of assistance from a school principal, as well they might. But improving the instructional program means changing it, which is an inherently disruptive but necessary process if a school is to be effective over any extended period of time. An effective principal does both jobs well: he helps teachers by providing the environment and tools to stimulate learning, and he tries to bring about planned change and to prevent harmful, unplanned change.

RESPONSIBILITIES AND COMPETENCIES OF SCHOOL PRINCIPALS

There are eight key responsibilities or broad functional categories in the carrying out of an effective instructional program. The school principal must see that these are carried out, but he does not work alone. The principal of the future will probably be less directive in his relationships with teachers and become increasingly adept at drawing the best out of others by using a collegial problem-solving approach. He will delegate, coordinate, stimulate—whatever is necessary to get the job done—but these are the categories of work that need to be performed, and the principal must see that each key responsibility is met.

Within each key responsibility area there are two or more competencies, which are defined here as the smallest unit of behavior that, if employed at a quality level, will make a discernible difference in the fulfillment of the responsibility. More specific behavioral manifestations of each competency are suggested, but these are only illustrative. They would not, standing alone, satisfy the requirement that there be a discernible difference in the fulfillment of the responsibility.

Some further comments about these behavioral manifestations of competency, called illustrative indicators, might be helpful. They are stated in *process* rather than *product* terms, although most of them could have been stated as products with only slight alterations in wording. Processes are suggested, even granting that product does not necessarily follow process as the night the day, for two reasons: since the major purpose of the evaluation is to assist school principals to improve their performance, the only available means of accomplishing this is to influence what the principal does; and what might appear to be the products of principals' leadership behavior might be affected by many other concurrent forces. To be sure, the effects of processes on outcomes must, ultimately, be considered, and relevant evidence pertaining to the outcomes of performance should be sought and taken into account. For example, Illustrative Indicator 23b, a laboratory session on teacher-made tests, is based on an analysis of the teachers' examinations using the Teacher Question Inventory. Two processes are in evidence here: the study of the examinations and the laboratory session that followed. The principal in this case should want to continue to collect evidence on the kinds of questions teachers use in their examinations to discover whether any changes are being made, whatever the causes might be, as suggested in Illustrative Indicator 28a. The immediate concern in evaluating the principal's performance is with what the principal does.

Illustrative indicators have been stated in the past tense; they could have been stated in present tense as well. The reason for stating each example as something the principal has done (or is doing) is to emphasize the point that sound evaluation must be based on the principal's actual behavior, not on something he is thinking about doing or on some trait he is presumed to possess.

High-priority expectations must be set periodically for certain broad categories of positions in the school district (elementary principals and secondary principals, for example) and for individuals in each particular situation. Not only do people, times, and situations vary, but role differentiation by positional categories must be provided if a school district is to make the most of its always limited resources. In order to get a "feel" for the priorities that might be set by practitioners, several school principals and instructional supervisors in the Houston public schools were asked to do a quartile ranking of the 32 competencies* presented in this chapter. The instructions were: "For each of the following competencies, indicate your estimate of its importance with regard to the effective performance of *your job* as an *instructional leader* during the next school year." Although generalizing from this limited sample would be hazardous, the results indicated that, for this group (twenty-four elementary and eleven secondary principals and fourteen supervisors), there are some

*Competencies 23 through 27 were revised slightly since they were presented to the Houston group, but they appear in Exhibit 1 substantially as they were stated at that time.

interesting commonalities and differences as a function of the position held. The following table shows the ten highest-ranking competencies for each of the three groups:

Rank	Elementary principals	Secondary principals	Instructional supervisors
	(Numbers refer to competencies, Exhibit 1)		
1	6	1	28
2	1	2	3
3	24	19	14
4	7	23	1
5	2	26	13
6	26	24	12
7	19	29	23
8	3	20	24
9	20	22	16
10	21	21	6 & 15 (tie)

Only two competencies (1 and 24) were in the top ten for all three groups. Several competencies (28, 14, 13, 12, 16, and 15) were in the top ten for supervisors only; one (7) was in the top ten for elementary principals only; and two (29 and 22) were in the top ten for secondary principals only. Five (2, 19, 20, 21, and 26) were in the high-ranking group for both elementary and secondary principals but not for supervisors. Several competencies were not among the top ten for any of the three groups' rankings.

The point in presenting these findings is not to argue that the method used in soliciting the opinions of the Houston group is an advocated procedure for arriving at a consensus for determining roles; in fact, such a procedure would be far too limited and superficial for such a purpose. The findings do, however, suggest the hypothesis that the administrative or supervisory position that one holds does influence his perceptions of the responsibilities that are most important. The contention here is that role differentiation is indeed important and should be accomplished in some deliberate and defensible manner. Efforts should be made to eliminate undesirable gaps and overlaps so that energies can be concentrated on the competencies that really count for a given position at a particular time, and individualization by personal and situational differences can then be added to complete the evaluation target for the individual principal. Early in each school year he can meet with an evaluator from the central office to review the goals and expectations held by the school district for the position, add goals that are unique to the individual, and proceed to state specific objectives for the school year. Many of the illustrative indicators, given in Appendix A to show the type of behavior that could be cited after the fact to suggest competency, could be stated as objectives. For example, a principal could state as objectives: "to initiate a study of diagnostic tests . . ." (No. 1a), "to develop a modular schedule . . ." (No. 10b), "to organize a 'scrambled' period . . ." (No. 11a), and so forth. Periodically during the school year the principal and the evaluator should meet to review progress and feed back the results of formative evaluation into the system. Objectives that are not reached at the end of the school year can be abandoned, revised, or carried over to the next year. See Appendix B for a suggested form.

The concrete evidence of performance required to make certain formal judgments about the principal would be much the same as that required to help him improve. The major differences would be that, for strictly judgment-making purposes, self-evaluation would probably not be appropriate, the results of others' evaluative judgments would probably not be revealed to the principal except in crisis situations (since such procedures are among the major causes of leniency error), and the evaluating would probably be infrequent rather than continuous. The format for this type of activity might simply be as shown in Appendix C, where the crucial competencies are stated in the column at the left, followed by a listing of specific evidences (more fully backed up in the principal's personnel folder) or a mark indicating "no evidence," followed by some sort of judgment about performance. If there is no evidence concerning a given competency, there can be no judgment about it.

One final suggestion is in order. The implications of a process such as the one proposed here could be so staggering as to immobilize even the best-intentioned administrator, or, even worse, a realization of what good evaluation and on-the-job training absolutely require might cause a retreat to the traditional ratings-based-on-hunches approach. It is doubtful that any school system can, in one triumphant stroke, adopt and operate a complete evaluation system for even this single domain of school principalship. How much better it would be to spend perhaps a year getting the necessary commitments, determining needs, setting goals, and training people to do the job—and then to start modestly and enthusiastically with some significant but manageable part of the job. The confidence that grows out of the attainment of limited but substantial objectives in the beginning can later support "going for broke" with much greater likelihood of success.

APPENDIXES

A. A LIST OF KEY RESPONSIBILITIES, COMPETENCIES, AND ILLUSTRATIVE INDICATORS

Key Responsibility I

The principal* develops school unit goals and objectives to guide instruction.

Competency No. 1: The principal relates needs of students to school system goals and legal requirements.

Illustrative Indicators

a. The principal initiated a study of diagnostic tests in order to select appropriate tests to identify specific needs of individual students.
b. The principal stimulated the guidance and counseling staff to conduct a survey of needs as perceived by the students.
c. The principal recommended a modification in school district goal X to accommodate a need of many students as revealed in a study of mental health problems.
d. The principal took action to correct a deficiency in meeting curriculum requirement X of the state department of education.

Competency No. 2: The principal defines goals and objectives that are unique to the school unit.

Illustrative Indicators

a. The principal appointed a committee charged with the responsibility of making an annual study of school unit goals and objectives and recommending changes to the faculty.
b. The principal compared demographic data pertaining to the school district as a whole with data for the school unit.

---

*The reader is again reminded that the principal is perceived to be a *leader* in the discharge of the responsibilities listed here, and not a lone wolf. Although each statement begins with "the principal . . ." since it is the principal whose performance is being evaluated, it is assumed that an effective principal will work with teachers and others in a supportive, nondirective mode.

Competency No. 3: The principal guides the development of instructional units to implement unique goals and objectives.

Illustrative Indicators

a. The principal assigned to a curriculum committee the task of developing an instructional unit to deal with mental health problems (as revealed in 1c, above).
b. The principal appointed a task force to develop instructional units on Negro contributions to American culture (as revealed in 1b, above).

Competency No. 4: The principal articulates goals and objectives for subunits within the school.

Illustrative Indicators

a. The principal required each department in the school to state its goals and to specify performance objectives under each goal.
b. The principal set up an interdepartmental committee to study goals and objectives (as stated in 4a, above) and to make appropriate suggestions to eliminate gaps, overlapping, and problems related to sequence.

Key Responsibility II

The principal allocates staff personnel to accomplish instructional goals.

Competency No. 5: The principal defines job requirements for each position in terms of instructional processes.

Illustrative Indicators

a. The principal initiated a study of the effectiveness of various instructional processes in producing each of several specified outcomes.
b. The principal interviewed two authorities on learning to discover the relationships between maturity and capacity to learn.

Competency No. 6: The principal assists in the recruitment and selection of personnel for instructional responsibilities.

Illustrative Indicators

a. The principal submitted job specifications (as indicated in 5a and b, above) for three vacancies that existed on his faculty.
b. The principal interviewed seven candidates for a position in his school to get evidence that they met all of the stated criteria (as indicated in 6a, above).

Competency No. 7: The principal assigns or reassigns instructional staff to optimize conditions for learning.

Illustrative Indicators

a. The principal provided tangible evidence of having matched individuals' competencies with specific job requirements (as stated in 6a, above) in the assignment of three teachers.
b. The principal reassigned a teacher to a position as chairman of the instructional media production team on the basis of skills she had acquired in a summer institute.

Competency No. 8: The principal recommends staff members for re-employment, promotion, or dismissal.

Illustrative Indicators

a. The principal recommended the dismissal of a teacher and supported the recommendation with a written analysis of the teacher's performance over a
period of three years, with substantial supervisory assistance as revealed in
written records of classroom observations using suitable guides, analyses of
students' test performances, and complaints from parents.
b. The principal justified the recommendation for re-employment of each teacher with written evidence of competence in the accomplishment of performance objectives.

Key Responsibility III

The principal allocates time and space to accomplish instructional goals.

Competency No. 9: The principal inventories the changing needs for time and
space for various instructional purposes.

Illustrative Indicators

a. The principal initiated the schedule-building process with a faculty discussion
of the time and space implications of the school's goals and objectives.
b. The principal worked with each departmental chairman to determine whether
new programs would require new allocations of time or space.

Competency No. 10: The principal allocates time and space to various instructional purposes.

Illustrative Indicators

a. The principal developed a class schedule that was unique to the school, reflecting the school's unique goals and objectives in four specific ways.
b. The principal developed a modular schedule that accommodated the special
needs of each subunit in specified ways.

Competency No. 11: The principal assigns students to appropriate spaces and
time units for instruction.

Illustrative Indicators

a. The principal organized a "scrambled" period one hour each week, during
which time groups of students from various grade levels received instruction
to meet specifically diagnosed needs.
b. The principal devised a plan whereby new students would be assigned to
homerooms with designated "buddies."
c. The principal changed the class section assignments of thirteen students during the semester, upon evidence that they would perform better in different
sections.

Key Responsibility IV

The principal develops and utilizes materials, equipment, and facilities to accomplish instructional goals.

Competency No. 12: The principal inventories the changing needs for materials, equipment, and facilities to accomplish instructional goals.

Illustrative Indicators

a. The principal established a system for developing the annual budget for materials, equipment, and facilities by having each subunit justify its requests in terms of expected outcomes of instruction.
b. The principal studied the results of standardized achievement tests and wrote an analysis of evident needs for instructional materials based on the test results.

Competency No. 13: The principal allocates materials, equipment, and facilities to accomplish instructional goals.

Illustrative Indicators

a. The principal presented a request for the purchase of a portable video tape recorder to be used in a proposed project aimed at helping teachers to analyze their own and others' teaching behavior.
b. The principal, because of disappointing student performances in reading comprehension in the primary grades (as revealed in 12b, above), ordered five extra supplementary books per pupil for next year.

Competency No. 14: The principal directs the identification and selection of needed materials, equipment, and facilities for instruction.

Illustrative Indicators

a. The principal asked each grade-level chairman to work with her group to identify and recommend for selection those materials best suited to the stated goals and objectives of the grade.
b. The principal charged the Library Committee with responsibility for reflecting school goals and objectives in the selection of library books and other instructional materials.

Competency No. 15: The principal coordinates the redesigning of instructional facilities to accomplish instructional goals.

Illustrative Indicators

a. The principal wrote specifications for the remodeling of the cafetorium so that it could be used more effectively as a night school learning center.
b. The principal worked with a graduate student in a study of the utilization of the language laboratory and recommended several specific actions as a result of the study.

Competency No. 16: The principal assists in the development or modification of instructional materials that are not available commercially.

Illustrative Indicators

a. The principal assigned an administrative intern the task of setting up a system for locating, assembling, organizing, and distributing noncommercial instructional materials.

b. The principal organized a series of in-service training sessions on the production of instructional materials.

Key Responsibility V

The principal coordinates supporting noninstructional services to accomplish instructional goals.

Competency No. 17: The principal inventories the changing needs for noninstructional services in order to accomplish instructional goals.

Illustrative Indicators

a. The principal worked with a group of graduate students in conducting case studies of five "problem" students, to determine possible relationships between their learning difficulties and their health and eating habits.
b. The principal asked the PTA to appoint an advisory committee to make a study of possible hazards to safety and other impediments to learning in and around the school and to make recommendations.

Competency No. 18: The principal organizes and coordinates the noninstructional services to optimize the accomplishment of instructional goals.

Illustrative Indicators

a. The principal changed the bus schedule so that students could participate in late-afternoon activities.
b. The principal organized a program of faculty-student lunches at which small groups would carry their trays to vacant classrooms and hold informal discussions during an extended lunch period.

Key Responsibility VI

The principal develops school-community relations to accomplish instructional goals.

Competency No. 19: The principal establishes communication with the school constituency for the purpose of assessing needs and setting broad instructional goals.

Illustrative Indicators

a. The principal organized an opinion survey, one section of which dealt with perceived shortcomings in the school program.
b. The principal wrote to business leaders in the community, asking them to project their employment needs for high school graduates for the next five years.

Competency No. 20: The principal explains school and school district instructional policies and procedures and reports instructional problems and achievements to the school constituency.

Illustrative Indicators

a. The principal explained school problems and achievements to seven lay groups in the community during the first semester.
b. The principal wrote a column for the local newspaper each week, dealing with some aspect of the school program.

Competency No. 21: The principal provides an adequate system for reporting students' performances to parents, prospective employers, higher educational institutions, and others.

Illustrative Indicators

a. The principal organized a study of the school's report cards, resulting in the addition of criterion-referenced measures.
b. The principal set up a schedule of teacher-parent interviews dealing with the accomplishments of students.

Competency No. 22: The principal communicates to the professional staff at school and district levels the feelings and desires of the school constituency.

Illustrative Indicators

a. The principal prepared a written report of community opinions concerning the school program (as revealed in 19a, above) and sent a copy to each faculty member.
b. The principal called a meeting of the faculty for the purpose of discussing means of preparing students for projected local employment opportunities (as revealed in 19b, above).

Key Responsibility VII

The principal develops in-service training programs to improve instruction.

Competency No. 23: The principal plans in-service training programs for teachers by relating performance data to school goals.

Illustrative Indicators

a. The principal organized a one-day, in-service training program in which small groups of teachers were guided into various specific activities on the basis of knowledge deficiencies as revealed in a pretest on different aspects of learning theory.
b. The principal conducted a laboratory session on teacher-made tests as a result of a study of the faculty's semester examinations, using the Teacher Question Inventory.

Competency No. 24: The principal guides individual teachers toward selective participation in in-service training activities.

Illustrative Indicators

a. The principal held an interview with each teacher during September for the purpose of cooperatively setting goals for the school year.

b. The principal assisted a teacher in selecting appropriate courses to take toward a master's degree, based on an analysis of classroom observation records over a period of one year.
c. The principal used the Mager-Pipe model in analyzing the performance problems of six teachers.

Competency No. 25: The principal leads in-service training sessions for teachers.

Illustrative Indicators

a. The principal organized and led a group of teachers in a visit to a demonstration school.
b. The principal asked the counselor to keep a record of various aspects of group participation at each faculty discussion, and this record served as the basis for one in-service session on group processes.
c. The principal conducted a laboratory training session for teachers (as in 23b, above).

Competency No. 26: The principal organizes and coordinates in-service training programs so as to make maximally effective use of personnel, time, materials, space, and money.

Illustrative Indicators

a. The principal used Instrument 6p-3, "Planning Worksheet for In-Service Sessions," in planning a summer workshop.
b. The principal surveyed in-service training offerings available through the central office, the local colleges, and the regional education service center and coordinated these offerings with the program in his building.

Competency No. 27: The principal trains other members of the professional staff to assume leadership roles in the in-service program.

Illustrative Indicators

a. The principal worked with department chairmen in a training program on classroom observation techniques.
b. The principal conducted training sessions for faculty team leaders in techniques for leading team planning sessions.

Competency No. 28: The principal assesses the effectiveness of in-service training activities and programs.

Illustrative Indicators

a. The principal followed up the laboratory session on teacher-made tests (see 23b, above) with an analysis of the teachers' next semester examinations.
b. The principal met with each teacher in November or December to check on progress made toward reaching goals set in September (see 24a, above).

Key Responsibility VIII

The principal assesses the needs of the school unit and evaluates the processes and products of instructions in order to improve instruction.

Competency No. 29: The principal collects, organizes, analyzes, and interprets data concerning the performance of teachers.

Illustrative Indicators

a. The principal used the Comprehensive Observation Guide with every first-year teacher at least three times during the school year.
b. The principal initiated a project in which a university supervision class visited a random sample of the teachers' classrooms, and, using the Comprehensive Observation Guide, they prepared a profile of the results for the faculty as a whole.

Competency No. 30: The principal collects, organizes, analyzes, and interprets data concerning other-than-teacher influences on learning.

Illustrative Indicators

a. The principal suggested to the Modern Problems class that it conduct a study of the community and its other-than-school opportunities for learning and report the results to the faculty and the students.
b. The principal initiated a study of peer preferences among students and used the results for planning and scheduling purposes.

Competency No. 31: The principal collects, organizes, analyzes, and interprets data concerning the performance of students.

Illustrative Indicators

a. The principal made a systematic study of student discipline referrals, their causes, and the teachers involved, and used the results in planning constructive programs with teachers to deal with the causes.
b. The principal enrolled in a Saturday course at the university and analyzed his students' performances on a standardized achievement test as a class project.

Competency No. 32: The principal collects, organizes, analyzes, and interprets data concerning former students.

Illustrative Indicators

a. The principal made a follow-up study of the employment record of last year's graduates and discussed the results with the faculty.
b. The principal used the performance of students who had gone from his elementary school to junior high school in the past four years as the basis for a faculty study of possible modifications in the curriculum.

B. SCHOOL PRINCIPALS' IN-SERVICE GROWTH AGREEMENT

Name of principal _____ Position _____

Assignment (school, project, etc.)_____ Date _____

High priority competencies	Objectives for school year 197 - 197
No.	
No.	
No.	
No.	
No.	
No.	

_____ _____ _____ _____
Signature of evaluatee   Date   Signature of evaluator   Date

FIGURE 6-1. School principal's in-service growth agreement form

C. EVIDENCE CONCERNING PRINCIPALS' PERFORMANCES IN HIGH-PRIORITY COMPETENCY AREAS

Name of Principal _____

School year _____

Competency	Tangible evidence (either state evidence or check "no evidence" and proceed to the next competency)	Judgment of performance[a]				
		A	B	C	D	E
No.	No evidence ____					
No.	No evidence ____					
No.	No evidence ____					
No.	No evidence ____					

_____   _____
Signature of evaluator   Date

[a]Key: A (completely unsatisfactory); B (needs much improvement); C (needs some improvement); D (satisfactory, but not outstanding); E (outstanding and exemplary)

FIGURE 6-2. Form summarizing principals' performance in high priority competency areas

NOTE

1. For example, see John C. Croft, "The Principal as Supervisor: Some Descriptive Findings and Important Questions," *Journal of Educational Administration*, 6 (No. 2, October 1968), 162-72; Wendell William Wolfe, "A Study of the Laboratory Approach to In-Service Development Programs for School Administrators and Supervisors," doctoral dissertation, University of Texas, Austin, 1965, pp. 136-54; Harry Jesse Gardner, "A Re-Study of a Laboratory Approach to In-Service Development Programs for School Administrators and Supervisors," unpublished master's thesis, University of Texas, Austin, 1968, pp. 57-73.

SEVEN

EVALUATING SCHOOL PROCESSES AND PRODUCTS: A RESPONSIBILITY OF SCHOOL PRINCIPALS

Dale L. Bolton

One of the many responsibilities of school principals is evaluation of teaching personnel, that is, making judgments regarding whether the procedures teachers use accomplish specified outcomes. The procedures are often referred to as processes, and the outcomes may be referred to as products. The principal is, therefore, responsible and generally held accountable for evaluation of school processes and products.[1] Stated another way, the principal must evaluate the procedures teachers use within a school as well as the results of these procedures in terms of student learning. Although the principal is responsible for this evaluation, this does not imply that all tasks described in this chapter are done by him. Rather, he is responsible for seeing that they are done. For example, in some large schools assistant principals and department chairmen may become involved in planning with teachers, collecting information, and conducting conferences with teachers.

Conceptually, evaluation of school processes and products may be viewed in a variety of ways. This chapter provides a brief description of several key concepts or features of evaluating processes and products, a discussion of the interrelationships of these key features and their implications, and a suggestion for managing information needed to evaluate a principal's effectiveness in this domain. The key concepts discussed are:

1. Evaluation[2] is a cyclical process of planning, collecting information, and using information.
2. Evaluation includes examination of input, process, and outcome.
3. Evaluation involves consideration of processes and products of several people.
4. Evaluation is a subsystem interrelated with other subsystems within the total school organization.
5. Evaluation procedures must determine direction, take action and acquire support, monitor processes and make intermediate decisions, provide support to the processes, and make terminal decisions.
6. Evaluation involves self-evaluation plus evaluation by outsiders.
7. Evaluation includes the assessment of common objectives and processes plus objectives related to a specific situation.

CYCLICAL PROCESS

Many people think of evaluation as an activity which occurs at a given point in time when a judgment is made regarding the value of a person's performance or the value of some product. Sometimes evaluation is perceived as the act of completing a form which expresses a summary judgment regarding activities or outcomes during a time period. Evaluation includes these summary judgments, of course, but to conceive of it solely in these terms is to ignore the major portion of the activity and several of its purposes (for example, the providing of systematic, frequent feedback so errors can be corrected) and to precipitate debilitating side effects such as negative attitudes on the part of the evaluatee.

Rather than being just a single phase, evaluation consists of multiple phases which are sequential, cyclical, and repetitive, and it builds on information and activities of the prior cycle. Because judgments are based on information collected, and because this information should be purposeful, the phases of evaluation may be considered to consist of:

1. "Planning for Evaluation," which involves analysis of a specific situation, establishment of purposes for evaluation, setting of specific goals and objectives, and deciding on means for measuring the processes used and the eventual outcomes.

2. "Collecting Information," which involves observation and monitoring of the activity planned.

3. "Using Information," which includes communication regarding the analysis and interpretation of information as well as making decisions regarding next steps to be taken.

The third phase becomes a natural prelude to the first phase, and the cycle is repeated. The information analyzed during the third phase provides the basis for reviewing the situation and resetting goals and objectives. This process is depicted in Figure 7-1.

Phase I: Planning for Evaluation

Examination of the situation which exists provides information necessary for making decisions regarding the purposes of evaluation, suitable goals and objectives, and the type of measurement which is appropriate. Minimal considerations should include the type of neighborhood being served, the nature of the students, the type of learning environment and facility, the traditions of the particular school, and the type of faculty and support system available.

The purposes of the evaluation system[3] are multiple, rather than singular. Since the purposes of evaluation must be determined for specific local situations, rather than imposed by external experts, a definitive list which fits all situations cannot be recommended. Consideration should, however, be given at least to the following:

to change goals or objectives,

to modify procedures,

to determine new ways of implementing procedures,

to improve performance of individuals,

to supply information for modification of assignments,

to protect individuals or the school system,

to reward superior performance,

to provide a basis for career planning and individual growth and development,

to validate the selection process, and

to facilitate self-evaluation.

Many problems may be avoided by openly discussing all purposes rather than allowing some of the purposes to be considered as hidden agenda which emerge during the decision phase of the evaluation process. Accomplishment of purposes of evaluation is directly related to the commitment to the activities involved. But how is commitment obtained? Generally, commitment is a natural outgrowth of

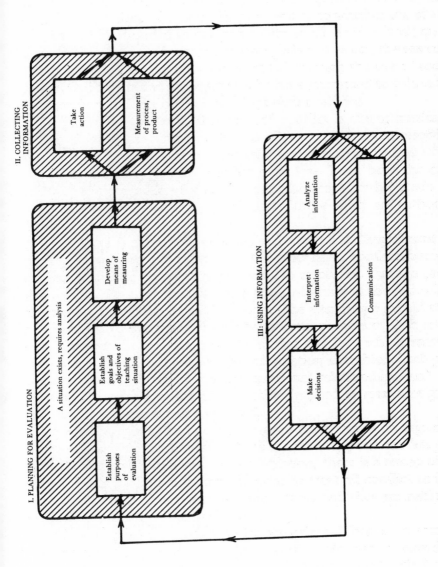

FIGURE 7-1. Evaluation of school processes and products:
A three-phase, cyclical process

agreement on purposes, and agreement on purposes is usually facilitated by open discussion among the people involved. Therefore, open discussion of the real purposes of evaluation tends to bring about agreement regarding these purposes and to alleviate fears that there are hidden purposes beyond those expressed.

Establishing goals and specific objectives for the teaching situation being considered involves a determination of what is important for that particular situation. Because a principal is responsible for what happens in a given building, he must consider the uniqueness of the building and the individual teachers and students within that building. In spite of the uniqueness of the specific situations, building goals must be compatible with district goals, and teacher objectives should be compatible with building goals. Because of these needs for compatibility and because of the divergence of views of people, the goal-setting activity must involve agreements and reconciliations regarding the appropriateness of targets. In addition, the setting of goals and objectives is not complete until agreements are reached as to what resources will be made available for the accomplishment of these objectives. In effect, it is one thing to agree that there should be a certain achievement by a given set of learners (a product or outcome) and that a given set of procedures will be used in order to accomplish this outcome. It is quite another thing to reach agreement regarding the resources which should be made available (such as audiovisual equipment, money for transportation for field trips, consultant help, and planning time) to produce the achievement desired. But well-established objectives include a consideration of resources needed to do the task. When agreements are reached prior to action, there is a much better chance that agreement can be reached regarding processes and products at the decision stage. For example, suppose that a given junior high school established a general goal of educating students regarding the hazards of drug abuse. The social studies department might decide to establish learning units on drugs, alcohol, and smoking for use with seventh- and eighth-grade students. Once the department had determined differences between the units to be used for the seventh and the eighth grades, a given teacher might then begin specifying the precise student learning desired for his classes (e.g., one of the objectives might be that 85 percent of the students will be able to list ten hazards of dope, alcohol, and smoking), the activities deemed necessary (for example, reading particular literature, listening to presentations, discussions, viewing films), and the resources needed (for example, funds for purchase of pamphlets, rental of films). Once objectives had been written and resources determined, agreements could then be made regarding whether the objectives were compatible with building and district goals, and of sufficiently high priority to warrant the use of the resources specified.

Developing means for measuring includes a determination of what information will be collected, an understanding of the limits involved in collecting data, and an agreement on the data-collection procedures to be used. Since either the principal or his assistants would be involved in collecting information regarding both procedures and products, a procedure for making decisions concerning outcomes in terms of student performance, teacher procedures, and principal procedures must be established. The important consideration at this point is to emphasize that the development of measurement should occur before action is taken (that is, before teacher procedures are implemented) and before information is collected. It is essential that the outcome should not influence the criteria for judging.

Consider also the teacher who is teaching the unit on drugs, alcohol, and smoking. Before the unit is begun, evaluators and teachers should agree on measurement of processes and products. Information regarding processes might include observation of a teacher presentation or classroom discussion and an examination of teacher records of activities such as viewing films. Measurement of product might include results on teacher-made tests, reactions to attitude questionnaires, observations of behavior of students at extra-class events, reports from others who observe students outside of school, or analysis of student discussions regarding the topic. The important idea here is not that there are specific measuring devices that are always appropriate to measure either processes or products, but that there is a need to determine what measurements are appropriate prior to implementation of the activities.

Phase II: Collecting Information

This phase consists of two parts: taking action or implementing procedures planned during the initial phase, and measurement of procedures and products, that is, collecting information regarding what happens during the action. In a school situation, the action consists mainly of teaching and supporting acts. Supporting acts by the teacher include those activities outside the classroom that are necessary to accomplish all of the tasks for which the teacher is responsible. In some locations this would include such things as explanation of programs to groups of parents, individual parent conferences, development of curricular materials and activities, and devising educational specifications for specialized portions of new school buildings. Supporting acts of the principal (or his assistants) include those activities that are designed to improve the processes of the teacher and that are necessary to provide the environment desired for students and teachers (see Figure 7-4).

Measurement during this phase includes the compiling of all information necessary to make decisions regarding whether goals and objectives have been accomplished. It includes such activities as classroom observation, out-of-classroom observation, administration of student tests, recording of student observations, acquisition of information from parents and students, self-report information from teachers, and recording of activities by means of audio and television recording devices.

Phase III: Using Information

This phase consists of the analysis and interpretation of information collected during the operation phase, and making decisions based on this information. Throughout the phase, there is communication between the principal (or his assistants) and teachers which helps them to decide whether objectives have been attained and whether changes should be made during the next cycle or time period.

Analysis and interpretation of information includes an examination of procedures used by teachers in the classroom and outside of the classroom, and by administrators in and out of classrooms; the information has, of course, been collected from many sources. Prior to this time, it has been possible to examine information regarding part of what has happened. If decisions are to be meaningful and helpful to the people involved, however, meaning must be attached to the total information collected, rather than following the often-used and erroneous practice of closure prior to careful and complete collection and analysis of data. During this interpretation process potential causes of problems can be identified as a result of the careful examination of procedures.

Analysis and interpretation of outcomes (results of the procedures followed) also occurs during this phase of the evaluation process. Teachers want to know whether student achievement, behaviors, and affective outcomes such as attitudes and interests were as great as the targets they set. On the other hand, principals are concerned with whether results of their in-service training and supervision were what they expected.

During this phase, decisions will be made regarding the following questions:

Were the outcomes (products) satisfactory?

Were the goals reasonable?

Were the procedures implemented as planned?

Were the procedures (as initially designed) effective?

What should be the next steps?

The first question involves a comparison of outcomes with initial goals. The second question involves a judgment regarding reasonableness, using the perspective of hindsight and all of the information regarding how the system performed after the goals were set. The third question involves a comparison of actual procedures with those planned during the first phase of the evaluation process. The fourth cannot be answered unless procedures discussed during the first phase were actually implemented; it, therefore, involves an examination of both procedures and products. The answer to the fifth question is based on complete analysis and interpretation of information regarding the product and process, and it includes a determination of whether to change goals, initiate controls over the implementation of the process, or change the procedures being used.

Let us revert to the example of the junior high school social studies teacher and the unit on drugs, alcohol, and smoking. Analysis of the information collected may indicate that certain cognitive objectives were met (for example, students may be able to list hazards of drugs), but observations of behavior may indicate that attitudes are such that approximately 20 percent of the students smoke regularly. If the objectives regarding attitudes toward smoking were such that the teacher desired less than 5 percent smoking, then the five questions listed above should be examined. Analysis of the information regarding procedures may indicate that certain planned activities may have considerable promise for changing attitudes and should be initiated.

INPUT, PROCESS, OUTPUT

An examination of the evaluation of processes and products of schools as explained in the prior section of this chapter indicates that it is closely allied to systems analysis procedures which examine input, process, and output. In systems analysis procedures, evaluation is made for the purpose of providing feedback regarding both process and output. Feedback is usually in terms of discrepancy, or differences between standards and actual performance. Since the discrepancy is concerned with both process and output, one of the necessities of evaluation in systems analysis procedures is establishment of standards. Such standards are established on the basis of a careful analysis of the input. Figure 7-2 illustrates a systems model involving input, process, and output.

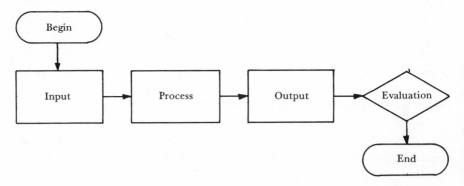

FIGURE 7-2. A systems model involving input, process, and output

The input stage is critical in terms of determining standards for both processes and output; the process stage is crucial because of the need to maintain process standards; and the output stage is important because one acquires evidence regarding whether he has accomplished what he desired to accomplish. But if the standards are established at the input stage, how is this accomplished?

Two types of variables are considered to determine the products desired: situational factors, and values. Two factors should be considered when determining what processes are likely to produce the outcomes desired: a logical analysis of the functions and tasks related to the outcomes, and an examination of what "good" personnel have done in similar situations. The relationships among these factors are illustrated in Figure 7-3.

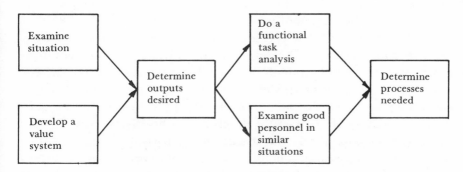

FIGURE 7-3. Relationships among factors related to output
and process standards

This figure illustrates the necessity of applying a value system to specific situational factors prior to determination of outputs desired (that is, output standards). Likewise, it illustrates the necessity of meshing the practical experience acquired by people in similar situations with the logic which a specialist (in curriculum or management, for example) might apply to a situation to determine what processes might be used. In lieu of information from successful practitioners and functional task analysis, some people make the error of asking all practitioners, regardless of how well they perform or whether they are in similar situations, to answer questionnaires about the efficacy of particular processes. Such information may be of questionable value when compared with that shown in the figure.

Again, let us examine the seventh-grade social studies unit on drugs, alcohol, and smoking. The value system[4] underlying the development of such a unit may express a concern for development of productive individuals who are contributing members of society. As the situation is examined, however, it may be determined that two major factors—widespread drug abuse and an unhealthy self-image—contribute to nonproductive citizens, and these two factors are interrelated. At the same time it is determined that some results or outcomes should improve the drug situation, there also might be some specific outcomes to encourage the development of healthy self-images of students. The determination of these desired outcomes represents an interaction of two elements: a value system concerned with productive citizens and a situation where problems exist in relation to both drug abuse and self-image (both of which are considered to be related to the value of productive citizens).

Once it is decided that the social studies department is also interested in contributing to the development of healthy self-images, how can processes be determined? The model indicates two concurrent steps: analyze the task to determine what functions should occur, and examine what "good" teachers do to develop healthy self-images. Analysis of the task of developing a healthy self-image may begin with an assumption that self-image is a part of a larger factor of general human relations. Therefore, one might work on the development of self-image within the general area of attempting to humanize education to the extent that respect for others—peers, people in authority positions, other races or ethnic groups—is developed. Our examination of "good" teachers may uncover the fact that many teachers who are successful in this area spend considerable time planning with students, considering their interests, and using their ideas to determine both goals and procedures for students. Following these determinations, the teachers (or principal or department chairman) may decide that completion of the major tasks involves two functions: interaction of students and teachers, and self-analysis of students. The interaction would require an examination and discussion of values in human relations (generally, and in relation to specific cases or problems), while the self-analysis would require some type of structured introspection.

Therefore, by examining what "good" teachers do, and by analyzing the functions of the task, it may be decided that the seventh-grade social studies teachers will use the following processes:

1. Include all students in the planning of the unit, considering their interests and concerns for goals and procedures for accomplishing these goals.
2. In planning and other class sessions, discuss values inherent in certain actions individuals take as they interact with others.
3. Design and use a guide to help students in doing a self-analysis of their own value systems in the area of human relations.

The example used illustrates one way outputs can be determined on the basis of a value system interacting with the peculiarities of a specific situation and how these outputs can lead to processes needed when functions of tasks are analyzed and the behavior of "good" personnel is examined.

Systems analysts are careful to propose that those who engage in one phase of the systems model are not necessarily those engaged in other phases. For example, individuals responsible for establishing standards at the input stage may not be responsible for completing the process; still others may have responsibility for evaluation and providing feedback regarding the process and output standards. The model itself does not suggest a division of labor which is likely to work across various situations, so such decisions must be made for each situation in a manner compatible with the total managerial style of the system.

SEVERAL PEOPLE'S PROCESSES AND PRODUCTS

When one considers the evaluation of school processes and products, it is necessary to realize that there are many products and not all personnel are working to affect these products directly. Whereas the teacher is directly responsible for outputs related to student behavior and achievement, the principal's procedures are only indirectly related to such products. Figure 7-4 illustrates the idea that some people's products are others' processes.

The significance of ideas embodied in the figure is that the functions and responsibilities of the principal are not focused directly on students. He may measure the discrepancy between his product standards and actual products in terms of processes used by the teacher rather than in pupil gain. This means that the direct desired output of his inservice program is to affect teacher behavior. He is also responsible for monitoring the teacher process-product relationship in such a manner that he knows whether teacher behavior is producing student changes that are desired by the school and the system, but such monitoring simply provides him with data which will help to identify differing teacher processes (his product) and principal processes which will have a high probability of assisting teachers in changing their behavior.

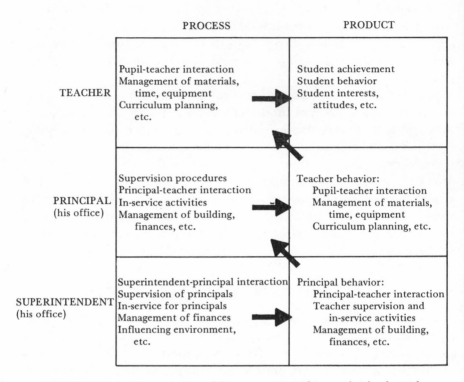

FIGURE 7-4. The relationship among teacher, principal, and
superintendent processes and products

Working directly with teachers to improve their teaching techniques does not encompass all of the responsibilities of the principal.
He is expected to produce outcomes in a variety of areas, and he is
expected to use a variety of processes. Figure 7-5 illustrates several
outcome areas and processes that are recognized as beneficial for attainment of objectives in these outcome areas.

Each cell of the figure represents an outcome area and a process
which might be related to it. By examining each cell of the figure, a
principal can identify the outcomes desired and suggest specific processes which might assist him in accomplishing these objectives. For
example, one of the cells relating to school-community relations is
that of communicating. This might involve newspaper articles, oral
reports to parents, and a regularly scheduled school newsletter coop-

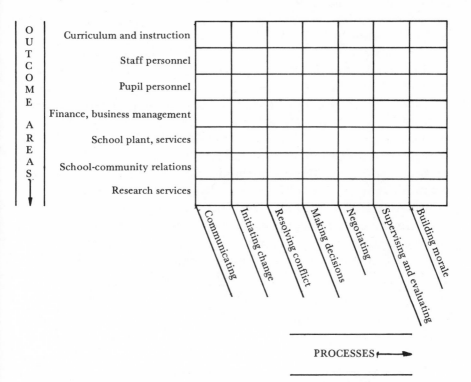

FIGURE 7-5. Outcome (product) areas and processes related to
responsibilities of school principals

eratively developed with the PTA. If a principal develops specific
outcomes that he considers important in this cell, then he and his
supervisor can determine whether the standard which was established
has been attained.

INTERRELATED SUBSYSTEMS

The evaluation process described in the first section of this paper
is interrelated with other subsystems within the total school system.
More specifically, one can examine the relationship of the evaluation
process described to other conceptions such as the management model, the learning cycle, and the personnel subsystem.

Concepts of management of school organizations have changed considerably during recent years. Many of the changes have involved a consideration of two central functions of administration, decision making and control. The use of control by administrators is considered by some to stifle creativity and initiative, repress behavior that might be beneficial to the organization, and perpetuate uniformity through fear of reprisals. This repressive connotation of the term "control" has received less attention in the posthuman-relations era. In contrast, the development of cybernetics has caused administrators to view control as a process of establishing dynamic equilibrium in the organization through reduction of deviation amplification.[5] Establishment of control in this context is accomplished by use of informative feedback (sometimes referred to as "neutral" to indicate its nonevaluative nature) to reduce deviation amplification in relation to desired goals.

The managerial cycle (planning, implementing, maintaining, and evaluating) illustrated in Figure 7-6 is a natural outgrowth of cyber-

FIGURE 7-6. Four phases of a managerial cycle

netic concepts and the use of feedback mechanisms for controlling organizations. The use of such a cycle serves two major functions: it provides the basis for individualized supervision practices, and it serves as a model for classroom teacher activities.

Although the learning cycle managed by the teacher is usually described as consisting of diagnosis, prescription, implementation, and evaluation (see Figure 7-7), compatibility of the two cycles is evident to most teachers.

Evaluation of personnel does not exist separately from other personnel functions. Therefore, one should not expect to understand the evaluation of processes and products of schools without examining the total personnel system. In analyzing the functioning of personnel systems, it is necessary to examine interrelationships of the selection, supervision, and in-service, and the evaluation subsystems.

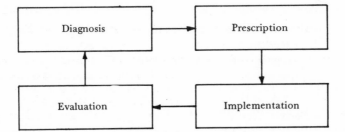

FIGURE 7-7. Four phases of a learning cycle managed by a teacher

While selection is based on a determination of needs for a specific situation, it provides a prediction of how an individual will perform and a determination of what type of supervision is appropriate for the person who is new on a job. Increasingly, the work of supervision and in-service training is being considered an individualized process based on information obtained from evaluation of performance as well as from the selection process. Evaluation, then, is related to each of the other two subsystems of the personnel system in that it provides feedback to make sure that the total system is functioning adequately. In the case of selection, it provides validation information; whereas, for supervision and in-service training, it furnishes information regarding needs of individuals so that assistance and decisions can be made appropriate.

PROVISIONS NEEDED IN AN EVALUATION SYSTEM

In order for an evaluation of school processes and products to be integrated with other subsystems and to contribute to the functioning of the total school system, there must be a means to:
>   determine direction,
>   take action and acquire support,
>   monitor processes and make intermediate decisions,
>   provide support to the processes, and
>   make terminal decisions.

Determining the direction of a school, a teacher, or a principal has been discussed previously in this paper and has received considerable attention in educational literature. It should be sufficient at this point to indicate that this involves specification of rather general goals or mission statements as well as more specific measurable objectives. The specific objectives are beneficial because of their implications for determining procedures.

Prior to taking action to accomplish goals and objectives, it is necessary to acquire material and psychological support for the action to be taken. Unless commitment is obtained for people, time, and material resources, action cannot be taken for planning—much less for implementation, maintenance, or evaluation. Commitment to support goals and objectives involves much more than simply encouragement to "go ahead and try it," or statements which imply that "I have no negative reactions to your proceeding with your plan." Such encouragement (or lack of discouragement) without commitment of resources may predetermine the results of evaluation of both processes and products at a later point.

Resources are needed to evaluate the end results or outcomes, but there is also a need to establish means for monitoring procedures so that intermediate decisions can be made and procedures can be changed before a summary evaluation. It might be necessary to monitor the planning, implementation, and maintenance procedures used by a principal before there is an evaluation of the total effect of his procedures on those with whom he is working.

Providing support to procedures (used by a principal, for example) while the procedures are still in use is a part of the maintenance function of the supervisor (or the principal). If the supervisor is maintaining that portion of the system for which he is responsible, he sees that his subordinates have the necessary staff, materials and equipment, and facilities to accomplish their tasks. This support is agreed upon during the planning phase, but the supervisor's management system should allow him to provide it at the appropriate time so that the subordinate can function effectively. A breakdown of such support will need to be considered as a contributory factor if there is a discrepancy between actual outcomes and the goals and objectives established.

Terminal decisions are simply those decisions made at the completion of a given cycle, as explained in the first section of this chapter, and they may be either positive, negative, or inconclusive. Terminal decisions are normally made at the end of a given time period (for example, at the end of a completed project, at the end of a school year), but they may be made prior to a normal terminal point if it is decided that the cost-benefit ratio is satisfactory. Regardless of when they are made, it is necessary that the evaluation system be designed in such a manner that there is adequate information to make a justifiable decision.

SELF-EVALUATION AND EVALUATION BY OTHERS

The trend toward self-evaluation has gained impetus from the teaching profession and the human relations emphasis therein. Consequently, its focus has been primarily on the process needed to accomplish objectives rather than on the objectives. This substitution of measurement of process for product has been justified by some on the grounds that the long-range goals of education are too difficult to measure, and the short-range goals are so difficult to attribute to causal factors that relating them to specific individuals' activities is unwarranted. The focus on procedures has been criticized on the basis that it makes unjustified assumptions regarding relationships between those procedures considered "good" and the results of the procedures; in effect, unless certain behaviors are known to produce certain results, very little benefit is obtained from evaluating behavior in isolation from the outcomes.

Since "pure" self-evaluation does not require an external observer in the measurement process, it has the advantage of reducing external threat and the potential for increasing creativity and motivation in comparison to situations where such external threat occurs. However, if the individual being evaluated (either a principal or a teacher) chooses to ignore district goals or to establish goals incompatible with those of the organization, to examine behaviors in isolation from outcomes, or to interpret data in a biased fashion because of prejudice or bias, he may do so under a system of self-evaluation. Therefore, self-evaluation has advantages and disadvantages.

To capitalize on initiative and creativity, individuals in an organization should be encouraged to develop systems of self-evaluation. However, to assure the organization that the goals, objectives, and procedures of personnel within the system are compatible with those of the organization, it is necessary that data be collected and analyzed by other individuals. Therefore, the system for evaluation of school processes and products should include means for self-evaluation and evaluation by outsiders.

COMMON AND SPECIFIC SITUATION
OBJECTIVES AND PROCESSES

People involved in educational research have sought long and hard for generalized statements regarding the effectiveness of teachers. They have spent less time in analogous research regarding effectiveness of administrators and supervisors, but it was the same reasoning that led to searching for the generally effective administrator. The results of these research efforts have caused research personnel to conclude that effectiveness in teaching and administration is more situation specific than generalizable. Therefore, more recent efforts have been made to determine the impact of situations on objectives desired, procedures used, and results of those procedures. In effect, more people are asking, "What works for me, in my situation?" or "What procedures do I need to use in order to obtain the results desired in this situation?" rather than "What is good administrative and supervisory behavior?" In order to answer this question for the specific situation, it is necessary to have good measures of both process and product; measurement of the product is necessary to determine if objectives were obtained, and measurement of the process is necessary to determine what produced the results and to decide on future actions.

This does not mean that it would be wise to abandon job descriptions of a general position, such as that of elementary principal, within a school system because there may be a number of responsibilities and tasks common to all people in that position. Such a job description might be quite beneficial to orient new principals or to evaluate commonly held responsibilities. Because of the lack of homogeneity of situations, however, there generally also exists the necessity to make a specific position task analysis in order to determine products and processes unique to that specific situation. Many school systems do not recognize this need, as evidenced by uniform reporting forms which do not have provisions for unique neighborhoods, children, staff, or learning facilities. Central office personnel may have reasonable justification for desiring some common criteria for judging effectiveness in relation to district-wide goals, but they should encourage principals to defend the uniqueness of their situation and the need for special evaluation procedures.

A SYNTHESIS

The discussion thus far has been concerned with the notion that evaluation is the process of making judgments regarding the value or "goodness" of certain behaviors, events, or results of events in terms of certain agreed upon or well-understood objectives. Notice that the implications of this definition include: (a) movement, indicated by the term "process," which has been described as having cyclical and iterative phases; (b) direction, established in terms of objectives; (c) measurement, a necessary element; (d) analysis and interpretation, preceding the attaching of values to processes or products.

Because of the complexity of the evaluation process, it has been approached in several ways (in terms of a general evaluation model, from a systems analysis perspective, in terms of its relationship to other subsystems, and so on). At this point it might be beneficial to synthesize what has been discussed by providing a relatively general model which includes elements of several of the previously discussed concepts, and a prototype form which might be useful in the early phases of evaluation for incorporating some of the necessary elements.

General Model

Figure 7-8 is an illustration of activities included in the evaluation of processes and products of a school. Note that it is basically a systems analysis model (including input, process, and output); that it includes the four elements of the managerial cycle; that the phases are sequential, cyclical, and repetitive; that it provides for intermediate as well as terminal decisions; and that it incorporates decisions regarding the appropriateness of goals as well as products and processes. Note that the model in Figure 7-8 does not specify the responsibilities of various people for the activities delineated because it is assumed that this must occur in a given situation. However, it is further assumed that the principal has the specific responsibility for managing the overall evaluation system. Likewise, he must determine the procedures whereby individuals are allocated responsibility within the total process. For example, consider the seventh-grade social studies situation in which we were concerned with drugs, alcohol, and smoking. It may be determined by the principal that the depart-

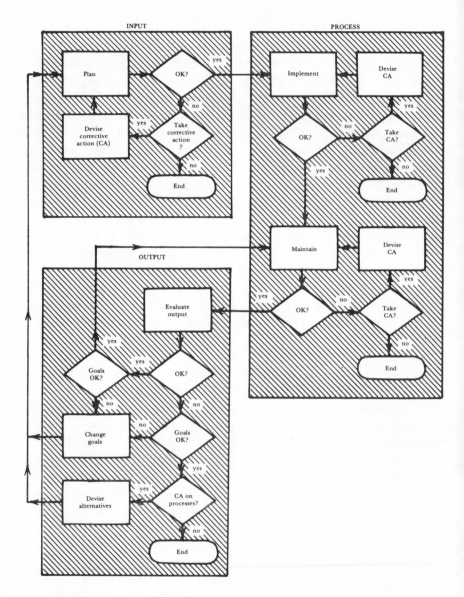

FIGURE 7-8. Activities included in the evaluation of processes
and products of a school

ment chairman and all of the social studies teachers should be involved in the initial planning in relation to the unit. In making a determination of whether the plan seemed feasible (or whether corrective action should be taken), however, the principal may decide that both he and the vice-principal should be involved in a discussion with the social studies department where the two decisions would be made. Many other options for involvement of the staff may be available to a principal. The collection and analysis of information necessary to make intermediate decisions regarding implementation or maintenance of the plant may be done by several people (principal, assistant principals, department chairmen, or teachers). However, the important point is that the principal has the responsibility for determining who should be involved, for structuring the decision process, and for managing the total sequence of events in the evaluation system.

Planning Form

The form that appears in the Appendix is suggested for use in one of the outcome areas for which a principal is responsible (program development). If completed by a principal and discussed with his supervisor, it would provide the stimulus for planning and the means for making decisions regarding measurement that would be necessary for both intermediate and terminal decisions.

The form has been completed to provide an example of how a principal might plan one aspect of program development to discuss with his supervisor. Since the actions needed for planning, implementation, maintenance, and evaluation are specified (along with information for monitoring the project), the principal and his supervisor can make intermediate and terminal decisions regarding his management of this objective. In addition, the specification of resources needed stimulates a reconciliation (if needed) of the priority of this particular objective in comparison with other objectives that require additional resources. Suggestions for types of items that could be developed for both intermediate and terminal decisions accompany the form.

The general model incorporates the following concepts:

1. Evaluation of the processes and products of a school is a cyclical process of planning, collecting information, and using information. (The form incorporates this idea by requiring evaluation at various stages of a project.)

2. Evaluation includes examination of input, process, and output. (Input on the form is considered by identifying goals and the resources needed for providing support; process includes all of the actions; and output is the statement of objectives and the information needed regarding accomplishment.)

3. Evaluation is a subsystem interrelated with other subsystems within the total school organization. (The management cycle of planning, implementing, maintaining, and evaluating is incorporated in the model. The form also incorporates this cycle with a means for monitoring the actions.)

In addition, the following concepts have been discussed:

1. Evaluation involves consideration of processes and products of several people. The position was taken that the principal should identify his product in terms of teacher behavior (teacher-pupil interaction, management of classroom organization, and so forth) and that his product therefore is the process of the teacher. (The form illustrates this concept.)

2. Evaluation procedures must determine direction, take action and acquire support, monitor processes and make intermediate decisions, provide support to the processes, and make terminal decisions. (The form illustrates how information can be obtained to facilitate this provision.)

3. Evaluation involves self-evaluation plus evaluation by outsiders. (The form and its attachment illustrate how information can be collected by a principal for his own self-evaluation, but the same information can be reviewed and shared by others in order to make decisions.)

4. Evaluation includes the assessment of common objectives and processes plus objectives related to a specific situation. (The attachment to the form illustrates how a principal might emphasize a particular aspect of his position, although such an objective may not be appropriate for all principals in a district for a given year.)

APPENDIX

PROGRAM DEVELOPMENT (CURRICULUM AND INSTRUCTION)

FOR DETERMINING DIRECTION

Project Goal: to provide leadership and assistance to teachers for individualizing instruction.

Objective: 1. (product) By April 15, 80% of the teachers will recognize the principal as an effective helper in individualizing instruction.
2. (process) Each teacher will be offered the opportunity to participate in an inservice activity which is designed specifically for him.

FOR TAKING ACTION AND ACQUIRING RESOURCES

Consider communications, decisions, conflict resolutions, negotiations, supervision and evaluation of personnel, developing morale, meetings, resources and time needed

FOR MONITORING PROGRESS

	Deadline	Indiv. Resp.	Information needed re accomplishment
Actions Needed for Planning:			
a. discussion with faculty	Aug 30	P*	minutes of meeting
b. discussion with departments	Sep 7	P,AP	minutes of meeting
c. discussion with individual teachers	Sep 20	P,AP,C	forms completed
d. meeting with curriculum administrator	Sep 15	P	letter of agreements
e. meeting with administrative council	Sep 21	P	minutes of meeting
Actions Needed for Implementing:			
a. meeting with departments	Sep 23	P,AP,C	minutes of meetings
b. initiate individual activities	Oct 7	P,AP,C	forms, letters
c. enroll teachers in inservice courses	Oct 1	C	forms
d.			
e.			
Actions Needed for Maintaining:			
a. observation of teachers in classrooms	**	P,AP,C	records and forms
b. confers with teachers	**	P,AP,C	written statement
c. keeps records of events observed	**	P,AP,C	forms, records, written statements
d. acquires materials, equipment	on request	AP	order forms
e.			

*Key: P: principal; AP: assistant principal; C: chairman, department or level.
**Deadline is determined according to a specified schedule.

Actions Needed for Evaluating:

a. teachers complete instrument	Dec 15 Apr 15	P	anonymous self-report device*
b. department meetings	Dec 15 Apr 15	C	written summary of discussion
c. analysis and interpretation of data	Dec 18 Apr 18	P,AP,C	minutes of meeting
d. cabinet meeting	Dec 20 Apr 20	P P	decision regarding next steps, minutes of meeting
e.			

FOR PROVIDING SUPPORT

Staff:

a. Special prerequisites needed: training and study in relation to individualized curriculum, including strategies to be used and materials deemed helpful.

b. Anticipated training needs: half of staff: workshop in writing objectives, designing activities; other half: diagnosis of their specific problems.
Approximate time: 3 days, 1 day follow   Approximate cost: $900

c. Additional staff needed: none at present
                 Approximate cost:

d. Consultant, supervisory help needed: Special consultant help from outside district on four days (suggest Mr. Otto Klever); regular consultant help as needed.   Approximate cost: see (b) above

Environment:

a. Special materials & equipment to acquire: Instructional materials in math, social studies: learning packets from Odscap
                 Approximate cost: $975

b. Adjustment or movement of materials, equipment: none at present
                 Approximate cost:

c. Special facilities needed: none at present
                 Approximate cost:

d. Adjustments to present facilities: install 20 carrels in library for individualized study   Approximate cost: $1300

*The anonymous self-report device might include items similar to those attached. It would be devised by the principal in conjunction with the assistant principal and the assistant superintendent.

ATTACHMENT TO PROGRAM DEVELOPMENT FORM

Teacher Reactions to Principal

INSTRUCTIONS: Please respond to the following items by placing a check (x) in the space you judge to represent your views.

1. Concerning knowledge and understanding of problems faced by classroom teachers, my principal

    understands   does not
    thoroughly ____ : ____ : ____ : ____ : ____ : ____ : ____ understand

2. Constructive criticism about my teaching offered by my principal is

    very   not
    beneficial   ____ : ____ : ____ : ____ : ____ : ____ : ____ beneficial

3. Discussion and conferences with my principal regarding my teaching (in relation to individualizing instruction) are

    very   not
    helpful   ____ : ____ : ____ : ____ : ____ : ____ : ____ helpful

4. When I have an educational problem concerned with individualization, my principal

    listens and   is not
    offers advice____ : ____ : ____ : ____ : ____ : ____ : ____ helpful

NOTES

1. In addition, the principal may have the responsibility for evaluating the productivity of the total school program (or a subunit of the school, e.g., the mathematics program), but the discussion here is concerned with productivity and processes of individuals.

2. Unless otherwise noted, "evaluation" refers to the making of judgments regarding both processes and products in terms of specified objectives.

3. Notice that the goals of the evaluation system are different from (though related to) statements of goals or objectives of the teaching situation. A goal of the evaluation system might be to improve the performance of individual teachers, while an objective of the teaching situation might be to develop specific interests or attitudes of students.

4. Such a value system may be a part of the Board of Education's philosophical statement, or an integral part of a given junior high school's statement of philosophy. However, the model itself is pertinent to an individual, and other examples might pertain to individual outputs which are determined on the basis of his personal value system combined with the situation within which he exists.

5. When an organization deviates from its objectives, or "goes off course," the deviation tends to enlarge unless some correction of error occurs. Control mechanisms are therefore used to reduce "deviation amplification" in order to keep an organization "on course."

EIGHT

PRINCIPAL PERFORMANCE: A SYNTHESIS

Max G. Abbott

This publication and the project from which it evolved represent a trenchant thrust in a profession that is still struggling to mature. The studies deal with six knowledge domains pertinent to the performance of elementary- and secondary-school principals. Unlike most previous efforts of this kind, however, these papers do not end with a summary of what is known. Instead, they present the implications of knowledge for practice, and they suggest evaluation procedures and measurement devices for assessing performance related to each knowledge domain.

The project was undertaken to suggest ways of assessing and improving performance. In doing this, the project and its resulting papers follow a trend established years ago in the study of educational administration, a trend enunciated by Halpin:

We will greatly increase our understanding of leadership phenomena if we abandon the notion of leadership as a trait, and concentrate instead upon an analysis of the "behavior of leaders."

What . . . do we gain by shifting our emphasis from leadership to the analysis of the behavior of leaders? There are two major methodological advantages. In the first place, we can deal directly with observable phenomena and need make no a priori assumptions about the identity or structure of whatever capacities may or may not undergird these phenomena. Secondly, this formulation keeps at the forefront of our thinking the importance of differentiating between the description of how leaders behave and the evaluation of the effectiveness of their behavior in respect to specified performance criteria.[1]

Admittedly, Halpin's reasons for maintaining a distinction between leadership as a trait and leadership behavior differed from the reasons for doing so in this project. Halpin was convinced that such a distinction was necessary if we were to increase our knowledge about, and understanding of, performance in the leadership role. The assumption underlying the current effort is that the same distinction needs to be made when the emphasis shifts from research—the acquisition of knowledge—to the application of knowledge for the improvement of practice. Though it may be interesting to know what causes people to behave as they do, the important consideration here is what type of behavior contributes to job effectiveness. The objective is not to change personalities, but to improve performance.

An individual cannot put to practice knowledge and concepts he does not possess; nor does the mere possession of knowledge and concepts ensure application. Our concern is with how principals perform, and performance is obviously the proper focus of attention. If, in an attempt to improve that performance, it becomes apparent that principals need to acquire new knowledge, this can be arranged. In the meantime, by concentrating on performance attention is directed appropriately toward helping principals improve their administrative skills, that is, their ability to apply to practice what they know.

When attempts are made to assess performance, it is essential to think in terms of effects. There is little point in attempting to alter an administrator's behavior unless there is reason to think that there will be some improvement in the organization. Yet, the requirement to point to the effects of administrative acts—to establish causal relationships between principals' performance and the successful functioning of their schools—confronts us with extremely serious problems. Little dependable, verifiable knowledge about such relationships exists.

This lack should not deter us, however, for the mere attempt to apply what is known will dramatize the fact that much more needs to be learned. A summary of available knowledge will, moreover, provide an excellent starting point for determining the directions to be taken in acquiring additional knowledge. The major, long-term contribution of the cooperative effort between the Atlanta public schools and UCEA may well be the research and development that it generates, but, in the meantime, efforts must be made to utilize what we already know. We can begin by clarifying the difference between the principal's role and the roles of other functionaries in the school. Bolton addresses this issue in Chapter Seven. His central thesis is that a principal's procedures are only indirectly related to student behavior and achievement. The direct, desired output of a principal's performance is, instead, improvement in the effectiveness of teachers.

Barnard's treatise of some fourteen years ago directly addressed the issue of executive functions in an organization. According to Barnard, "executive work is not that *of* the organization, but the specialized work of *maintaining* the organization in operation."[2] Thus, following Barnard, executive functions in a manufacturing firm do not involve designing the firm's products, participating in the manufacturing process, nor engaging in the sale of the finished products. Rather, executive functions consist of the procurement of resources and the providing of a framework for decision making, including decisions regarding what is to be produced, how it is to be produced and marketed, and how various parts of the firm relate to each other. To state it in more general terms, executive functions consist of activities that facilitate and coordinate the more technical functions of the firm. Executive success is gauged by how well other oganizational functions are in fact facilitated and coordinated.

Similarly, executive work in the school does not include teaching students, assessing pupil progress, nor reporting on that progress to parents. The effective school executive is concerned with how well these functions and others are carried out. He also has direct responsibility for seeing that the necessary resources for conducting the work of the organization are provided, for coordinating the various functions of the organization, and for seeing that the environment in which those functions occur is facilitative. Thus, as Bolton suggests, it is the principal's performance with teachers and other functionaries as a group—in relation to the organization—that provides the basis for determining his or her effectiveness.

When he discusses human relations (Chapter Five), Hughes presents a useful concept for thinking about the school as an organization and about those facets or variables affected by the principal's performance that make a difference in how the organization functions. Several terms could be used to refer to this concept, including those of "organizational health," "organizational climate," and "self-renewal." Whatever the terminology, the underlying concept suggests that certain conditions, if predominant in the organization, tend to be facilitative, while other conditions, if predominant, tend to be inhibitive. Two major questions arise: What constitutes a facilitative climate? What can a principal do to establish and maintain such a climate?

Two formulations in the literature are useful in examining what constitutes a facilitative climate. The first, developed by Miles, uses the term *organizational health* to refer to the organization's ability "not only to function effectively, but to develop and grow into a more fully functioning system."[3] Miles suggests ten dimensions of organizational functioning that together constitute such a state of health: goal focus, communication adequacy, optimal power equalization, resource utilization, cohesiveness, morale, innovativeness, autonomy, adaptation, and problem-solving adequacy. There is a striking similarity between Miles's formulation and the domain papers in this publication.

A somewhat different but useful formulation discussed by Hughes, the "Organizational Climate of Schools," grew out of the research of Halpin and Croft.[4] They developed six profiles ranging on a continuum from closed to open to describe the climate of schools. An open-climate school is described as a lively organization moving toward organizational goals while also providing satisfaction to its members. Such a school is characterized as having high morale; moderate intimacy, with teachers having neither an undue need for social interaction nor a desire to avoid such interaction; low disengagement, or a sense of being part of a unit in which energies are devoted to accomplishing the task; and low hindrance, or the relative absence of nonproductive busy work and trivia.

Although we do not have incontrovertible evidence that a school that conforms to either of the above formulations is clearly superior in terms of providing a good environment for learning, some empirical evidence, and a great deal of logic, suggests that this is a working hypothesis. Even if we accept such a hypothesis, however, it is still necessary to return to the second question raised above: What aspects of the principal's performance contribute to the establishment and maintenance of a facilitative climate in schools?

A useful way of thinking about administrative performance has been provided by Katz.[5] In developing his framework, Katz took a position similar to that of Halpin: "The quest for specific traits or qualities of an effective executive causes us to lose sight of our real concern: 'what a man can accomplish.' "[6] When we concentrate on what an executive can do—performance—we are concerned with "the kinds of skills which [executives] exhibit in carrying out their jobs effectively.[7] These skills, according to Katz, are conceptual, technical, and human.

CONCEPTUAL SKILLS

Of the three types of skills, conceptual ones are most directly associated with knowledge. To conceptualize, an individual needs both a store of information and a basis on which to order that information. Although they are dependent on knowledge, conceptual skills represent more than the acquisition of knowledge. If an individual possesses conceptual skills, he has developed the ability to apply information and concepts to practice. This involves the ability to see the organization as a whole and to understand how various parts of the organization relate to and affect each other, which requires diagnosis and analysis. Conceptual skills refer to the ability to discern meaning in and to establish relationships among events and bits of information that at first glance would appear to be discrete and unrelated.

Although conceptualizing permeates everything an administrator does, two major sets of activities in which all administrators engage require highly developed conceptual skills: making decisions and managing conflict.

Decision Making

Lipham defines a systems approach (Chapter Four) that includes five steps in the decision-making process: identifying the nature of the problem, determining solution requirements and alternatives, choosing a solution strategy from alternatives, implementing the solution strategy, and determining effective performance. All of these steps involve conceptualizing about past, present, and future events.

It is a rather simple step in logic, therefore, to conclude that effective decision making represents highly developed conceptual skills. This is much too simple to be useful, however. If an individual's effectiveness as a decision maker is to be assessed or improved, it is necessary to identify the particular skills that contribute to such effectiveness and to find ways to measure those skills and to increase the individual's ability to employ them. Such skills, suggested earlier in this book, include: differentiating among types of decisions, determining the amount and type of information needed to reach a decision, determining the appropriate involvement of other people in reaching decisions, establishing priorities for action, and anticipating both intended and unintended consequences of decisions.

Differentiating among Types of Decisions

Much of the literature on decision making reads as if all organizational decisions are similar and can be approached using the same procedures. This obviously is not the case. Because decision situations vary, the types of decisions that must be made do, also. Along with Griffiths, Lipham sees three major types of decisions—intermediary, appellate, and creative—requiring different information, procedures, and abilities on the part of the decision maker. There are other classification schemes that might be used to indicate the differences that exist among decisions made in an organizational setting.

Differences also exist among decisions that must be made in a school. For example, if a decision can be implemented only when it is fully understood and supported by a school faculty, that faculty obviously would need to be involved in making the decision. On the other hand, if a decision can be implemented merely through administrative action, particularly if the content of the decision is of little consequence to faculty members, then the involvement of the faculty wastes valuable time and damages faculty morale.

Variations in the amount and type of information needed to support a decision, the procedures that should be used to reach a decision, the individuals who should be involved in decision making, and the steps required to implement the decision once it is made must be considered whenever a decision situation arises. An administrator has to discriminate among issues and differentiate among types of decisions if the school is to take appropriate action.

Determining the Information Needed for Decision Making

Lipham has shown the importance of information in decision making, and pointed out that the search for information constitutes a significant first step when preparing to make a decision. The administrator who consistently makes decisions without adequate information frequently finds himself enmeshed in problems of his own making. He may initiate action to solve a problem that does not exist; he may fail to recognize a problem that literally clamors for attention; or he may perceive a problem so inaccurately that any action taken would be inappropriate. Gaynor illustrates the point in Chapter Three when he discusses the tendency of some principals to overreact to complaints from highly vocal but small groups of citizens while totally ignoring the concerns of large segments of the less vocal population.

Just as it is possible to err by taking action without adequate information, however, it is also possible to err by delaying action unduly in order to search for further information. Those who postpone decision making until *all* of the information is in need to be reminded that *all* of the information can never be assembled. Problem situations do not remain static; they change with the passage of time. It is never possible to know whether one has reached the best decision, only to determine whether one has reached a satisfactory decision. Thus, as March and Simon point out: *"decision making, whether individual or organizational, is concerned with the discovery and selection of satisfactory alternatives: only in exceptional cases is it concerned with the discovery and selection of optimal alternatives."*[8]

The effective administrator, then, has a good sense of when there is sufficient information to justify action. This involves judgment, of course, but it also involves skill, skill that can be increased through training.

Determining the Appropriate Involvement of Other People

Much of the educational administration literature has been confusing on the issue of employee participation in decision making. The writing on "democratic administration" has been particularly misleading, frequently conveying the impression that all employees have an inherent right to be involved in every decision made.

Both Lipham and Gaynor illustrate the fallacies that occur in such a situation. There are many reasons why employees should participate in decision making; indeed, such participation is essential if the full understanding and support of a school faculty is required for the successful implementation of a decision. Employee participation also reduces the visibility of power relations in an organization, thereby building up employee morale.

The fact remains, however, that decisions must occasionally be made without the direct involvement of employees. Sometimes this occurs because of an urgent need for action. At other times, the decision is of little direct interest to employees. Finally, some decisions are of such overriding importance to the management of an organization that they must be made from a managerial perspective, even at the risk of lowering employee morale.

An effective administrator must be able to make defensible judgments in this area. He should recognize when involvement is needed and when it is unnecessary, judge when participation is essential for implementation and when it is irrelevant, determine whether an issue is of unusual importance to management or whether this is simply a rationalization to avoid sharing decision-making prerogatives. Although it is unreasonable to expect any administrator to maintain a perfect score in this regard, it is reasonable to expect that serious errors will seldom occur. Because it is possible to improve an administrator's skill in determining the appropriate involvement of other people in decision making, it is also reasonable to expect that there will be an improvement.

Establishing Priorities for Action

One of the first facts of life that a new administrator discovers is that he will have more problems and issues brought to his attention than he can possibly deal with. Some will be crucially important, many will be trivial; some will require immediate attention, others can or should be deferred; some will require his personal attention, others can be delegated. Any administrator is frequently, if not constantly, confronted with the need to establish priorities. He can do so deliberately and with forethought, or he can allow priorities to be set haphazardly. However it happens, one thing is certain: priorities will be set.

The skillful setting of priorities involves much more than merely reviewing a series of items and establishing a time schedule for action. It requires the judicious use of information, some of which may be readily available and some of which will need to be assembled. It also involves skill in anticipating the consequences of acting immediately or of deferring action, of taking action personally or of delegating action to others. The sounding of a fire alarm indicates that action can be ignored or deferred only with extreme risk. On the other hand, a conflict between two teachers frequently, though not always, benefits from a period of benign neglect.

As is true in the case of other skills related to decision making, skill in setting priorities frequently increases with experience. As is true in the case of those other skills, skill in setting priorities can also be enhanced through the use of appropriately designed training activities.

Anticipating Consequences

As Lipham points out, decision making consists essentially of estimating the outcome state of a system. That is, reaching a decision involves making choices based on predictions of the probable consequences of alternative courses of action. No decision produces only one effect or set of effects, however. Nor are the consequences of a decision ever limited only to those intended. Initiating a course of action to solve one problem may create other problems; it may also generate an entirely different response than that intended.

One example of such a response can be found in the action taken by an elementary school principal to deal with the problem that arose when a few teachers in the school kept arriving late. The teachers involved failed to respond to informal reminders that they should be in their classrooms a reasonable period of time prior to the opening of school, so the principal announced a new policy whereby all teachers were required to report at least one-half hour before classes began and to remain at least one-half hour after classes were dismissed. Although the new policy accomplished the intended purpose, at least temporarily, it generated an unintended, undesirable response. Some teachers, who had consistently arrived on time and remained after school as long as was necessary to prepare for the following day, were so offended by the arbitrariness of the new policy that they remained only the required period at the end of the day and then left the school.

To take another example, Lortie relates the case of a high school principal who was puzzled at the resistance he encountered when he attempted to initiate a plan for curriculum revision. Although the plan was popular with the faculty and although the principal could detect no obvious weaknesses in the revised schedule called for by the plan, opposition persisted. It was discovered, on closer examination, that the new schedule had the unintended effect of disrupting the social interaction patterns of a group of respected and influential senior teachers. When the principal took steps to eliminate that feature, the plan was willingly accepted.[9]

These examples support literature on decision making in which heavy emphasis is placed on the consideration of alternatives. Lipham refers to input-output analysis as a means of weighing and comparing alternative courses of action. Such analysis consists of estimating both the benefits and the costs of each alternative and of choosing the solution strategy that promises to deliver the maximum benefits for minimum costs.

In using cost-benefit analysis, however, we must not overlook some of the most significant costs in human endeavors. While many costs associated with any set of activities—personnel, materials, facilities, and equipment—can be translated into dollars, other costs cannot readily be equated with money. Such things as lower staff morale, conflict, student unrest, and a high turnover rate cannot be easily converted to dollars. Yet these conditions represent real costs to the organization. At times they can be disruptive enough to virtually nullify other organizational effects, and they almost always occur as concomitant consequences of decisions intended to produce beneficial effects.

Two terms refer to these concomitant consequences of organizational decisions: unintended consequences and unanticipated consequences. As indicated earlier, all decisions produce unintended consequences. Whether or not these consequences create serious organizational problems, however, frequently depends upon whether they take the organization by surprise.

An accurate assessment of the probable consequences of a proposed decision greatly reduces the chances that an organization will be taken by surprise. In some instances such an assessment shows that unintended consequences have potential for serious disruption. With advance information, the organization is prepared to take steps to minimize or to counteract those disruptive effects. In other instances, the harmful aspects or unintended consequences of a proposed decision are judged to be so seriously harmful to the organization that the decision is never made. Such judgments cannot be made unless the unintended consequences are anticipated. A crucially important administrative skill is, therefore, the ability to elaborate and to make explicit the possible consequences, both intended and unintended, of each decision proposed, and of thus reducing to a minimum the unanticipated consequences of each decision reached.

Conflict and Conflict Management

Whenever two or more people join together in purposeful activity, the potential for conflict exists. Conflict, of course, is not necessarily dysfunctional; in fact, a substantial body of literature deals with the positive functions of organizational conflict. Whether a conflict situation turns out to be functional or dysfunctional frequently depends on an analysis of the forces involved and the response made to those forces.

To be effective, therefore, a school principal must develop the ability to analyze and diagnose conflict situations and to choose courses of action that respond both accurately and adequately to those situations. An inappropriate response to an emerging conflict can exacerbate that conflict; it does nothing to reduce it.

The analysis required for appropriate responses places heavy demands on an individual's ability to conceptualize. It is essential for the administrator to assess accurately the type of conflict with which he is confronted. At the same time, he must be able to determine the source of the conflict. In making such an assessment, it is useful to distinguish between conflict that occurs because of disagreements regarding goals and procedures and conflict that arises from performance requirements of organizational roles.

Conflict over Goals and Procedures

Following March and Simon,[10] interpersonal conflict may arise because of disagreement about goals and values or disagreement regarding actions to be taken in pursuing goals or implementing values.

All organizations require general agreement regarding goals and values as a unifying force. Whether an organization's primary goal is to maximize profit, eradicate disease, improve the environment, or educate children, that goal determines the organization's activities. Shared values provide the basis, moreover, for resolving differences that arise regarding the legitimacy of organizational demands on both employees and clients.

It is not surprising, then, that conflicts involving disagreements about goals and values are particularly troublesome. Recent controversies over sex education in schools represent a case in point. Those controversies have arisen not because of disagreements as to how sex education should be conducted, a procedural question. Rather, they have arisen because of serious disagreement as to whether sex education should be included in the curriculum at all, a value (goal) question. In the absence of agreement over goals and values, the sex education issue has consistently been settled through the use of social power. Opponents and proponents alike have attempted to gain sufficient support to force officials to adopt their positions.

To generalize the issue, this type of conflict is characteristically settled through bargaining or the use of power. Moreover, resolving this type of conflict almost universally involves a win or lose situation; for one party to gain, another must lose. Thus, both the conflict and the procedures for resolving it place considerable strain on organizational relationships, particularly those with an authority dimension.

When there is agreement on goals and values but disagreement regarding appropriate procedures, on the other hand, conflicts become far less traumatic and readily amenable to resolution through problem solving. Thus, when differences arise, information about possible alternatives for action should be sought. The alternatives should then be examined to determine the probable consequences of their adoption. Cost-benefit analyses could be carried out for each alternative, and choices should be based on the information assembled. Such procedures place little strain on organizational relationships, and the solution strategies adopted are generally designed to maximize gains and minimize losses for all concerned.

Because bargaining and power struggles place strains on organizational relationships and because those in authority positions feel particularly vulnerable in a win or lose situation, there is a strong tendency for administrators in organizations to treat all conflict as if it were based on disagreements over procedures and thus amenable to resolution through problem solving.

Such a response is frequently inappropriate. When fundamental disagreement over goals and values occurs, information regarding alternative courses of action and probable outcomes is largely irrelevant. Thus, while organizational resources are being devoted to information gathering, a largely futile activity, the conflict persists and exacts its own toll in organizational energy.

An effective administrator must, therefore, be skillful in determining the nature of any conflict. If it involves procedures, he can proceed in a problem-solving mode. If it involves goals and values, one of two courses of action may be appropriate.

One course may be to recast the conflict into a problem-solving mode, which can only be accomplished by recognizing and admitting that disagreements about values exist and by moving to a new level of values on which agreement can be reached. To cite an example, a few years ago a southern university was confronted with a court order to admit its first black student. The issue created pervasive and deep divisions. The board of trustees, the university president, and many faculty members and students were opposed to the court order, and, at the same time, some faculty members and a few students strongly supported it. Prospects for a major confrontation, with possible physical violence, were high.

The president went into action. He announced that on a given day all afternoon classes would be canceled and that a mass meeting would be held in the football stadium. Every member of the university community was urged to attend. At the meeting several presentations were made, but none dealt with the court order. That issue was treated as a given. Rather, appeals were made to preserve the reputation of the university. The strategy was evident: move from one set of goals and values, over which there was obvious and irreconcilable disagreement, to another set of goals and values over which it was possible to obtain agreement. This strategy was apparently successful in diverting the pending confrontation, and a conflict situation was handled, not by ignoring it but, rather, by translating it into a manageable context.

Not all conflict situations can be handled this way. Some simply cannot be, and others should not be. Another course of action would be to use bargaining and political action, thoroughly legitimate approaches to conflict resolution. Discomforting though these approaches may seem to those in authority, under certain conditions they represent the most appropriate approach available. Employed judiciously, they can be a means of moving the organization to a new level of functioning.

Conflict on Role Requirements

Administrators are constantly confronted with conflicts related to organizational roles and role performance. Because such conflicts tend to center around individuals, there is a general tendency to treat them as personality clashes. Such an approach is both simplistic and inaccurate, and its use does little to improve the situation. Only if an administrator can look beyond the personalities involved to discover the underlying causes of the conflict can he hope to succeed in resolving it.

Just a short time ago, two elementary school teachers were experiencing great difficulty in cooperating in a team-teaching arrangement. On the surface they appeared to be in general agreement regarding both the content and processes of instruction that were being used. Yet clashes continued to occur. After considerable inquiry the principal discovered that the two held widely differing views regarding appropriate pupil behavior. One took the position that students should remain orderly and quiet; the other held that a child's behavior should be challenged only if that child were disrupting the class or interfering with others. Through discussions with the principal and sharing their views with each other, the teachers came to recognize the source of the conflict. Having done so, they found that they understood each other better and that they could work together.

To deal with the variety of such conflicts that arise, it is necessary that the principal understand the source, some of the most important and frequent being differentiation or specialization, multiple expectations for role performance, and occupancy of multiple roles.

To take advantage of specialized training and abilities, organizations divide functions into specialized tasks. In schools, some teachers specialize in teaching mathematics; others, music; still others, art; and so on. While the quality of performance is thus generally increased, specialization creates a new set of problems. Individuals in specialized roles tend to equate the goals of the organization with the goals of their specialty. This can lead to conflicts with other units, particularly when there are competing demands on resources or facilities. Resolving these conflicts calls for great skill on the part of a principal. To treat them as personality clashes is futile and self-defeating. Somehow all parties to the conflict must be made to realize that the accomplishment of the organization's general goals requires the cooperative and additive performance of its specialized units. This approach not only ameliorates the conflict, but it frequently produces better ways to accommodate competing programs and to effect mutual improvement.

Regardless of the organizational role one occupies, there are always different groups who hold different expectations for performance in that role. Teachers, for example, may find themselves simultaneously trying to please the principal, supervisors, parents, and students. Although it is not possible to remove this source of conflict, it is possible to reduce its consequences greatly. The school principal is in a strategic position to serve as a buffer between teachers and parents, to moderate the excessive demands of supervisors, or to negotiate differences between teachers and students. A willingness to perform these roles, however, depends upon the principal's ability to understand and appreciate the nature of the conflict and its seriousness.

Just as individuals are subject to multiple expectations for performance in a given role, so also do they experience conflict because they occupy multiple roles. A teacher may also be a mother (or a father), and the demands emanating from the two roles may at times be seriously incompatible. A seemingly recalcitrant teacher may not be recalcitrant at all; she may be under serious pressure at home. An apparently uncooperative teacher may also be experiencing serious conflict because of incompatible demands between his teaching role and his role as president of the local teachers association (or union). Again, such conflicting demands cannot be removed entirely, but an understanding principal can do much to ameliorate the conflict.

The point of this discussion is that there are a number of concepts related to conflict that help in understanding and dealing with it. The effective principal needs such concepts, and he needs to apply them skillfully in a live setting. Training opportunities are needed to help principals develop such skills.

TECHNICAL SKILLS

Technical skills are related to methods or techniques of getting a job done. An accountant who organizes, manipulates, displays, and controls financial data well has developed the technical skills of accounting. Similarly, an administrator is called on to perform many tasks that call for highly developed technical skills.

Compared to conceptual and human skills, technical skills should be relatively easy to identify, assess, and develop. Yet, surprisingly little progress has been made in this respect during recent years. Perhaps this is because we rejected the earlier emphasis on administrative techniques or because we were preoccupied with the social sciences and their possible contributions to the field. In any event, renewed attention to this skill area is necessary if we are to improve the performance of the school principal.

Three categories of technical skills appear to have considerable potential for enhancing the performance of school principals: planning skills, group process and communication skills, and management skills.

Competent principals have employed a variety of techniques related to these three categories of skills for generations. Many have proven effective and will continue to be used, and some newly emerging technologies, such as electronic data processing, hold particular promise for the improvement of technical skills. These technologies, neutral in terms of human values, can be either humanizing or dehumanizing in use. They can lead, in the words of Harman, to a "person-centered" society or to a "second-phase" industrial society.[11] The choice lies with the user.

Planning Skills

Planning of some type is inherent in virtually all human activity. In schools, the establishment of budgets, the issuing of contracts, the purchasing of books and supplies—all represent routine actions undertaken as a part of planning for future events.

In recent years, the term "planning" has begun to take on a somewhat new and more precise meaning. Beginning with the trend toward applying systems concepts in organizational analysis, "planning" has come to imply a shift from an emphasis on processes to an emphasis on outputs as a means of assessing an organization's effectiveness. Involved in this shift is a demand for more explicit definitions of organizational goals, inputs, processes, and outputs, and for a more careful monitoring of processes to improve the output-input ratio.

With the emphasis on improving administrative performance in relation to organizational goals, the preceding chapters and the project that prompted them conform to this new trend. McIntyre's list of the principal's key responsibilities (Chapter Six) begins with the establishment of goals and objectives to guide instruction. Most of the other responsibilities in that list refer to activities designed to improve the organization's performance in respect to those goals. Bolton's approach to evaluating school processes and products likewise deals with ways to use the outcomes of instruction as the basis for assessing and improving instructional processes, which, in turn, is expected to improve the school's performance in relation to its goals. Finally, Lipham's study of decision making is organized around systems concepts, with heavy emphasis on the use of objectives and information feedback in managing the decision-making process.

Planning in this new mode will not occur merely by changing terminology, however. If planning within schools is to differ substantially from that of the past, school principals must learn to use new techniques and know when to use the most appropriate ones. These new techniques include using input-output analysis to improve organizational processes and to assess the community that the school attempts to serve.

PPBS

One promising approach to improving organizational processes with the aid of input-output analysis is through Planning, Programming, Budgeting Systems (PPBS). PPBS is more than a technique; it is a technological system that incorporates many techniques. It is, however, a manageable system, and increasing evidence suggests that it can be adapted for school use with salutary effects.

One such system, designed explicitly for use in schools and currently being implemented in a school district, consists of six major phases of activity.[12] Phase one, a systems analysis phase, identifies a school's ongoing activities at the level where intensive program planning takes place. Phase two consists of a cost-accounting system developed to monitor both actual and desired inputs to the school. In phase three, operating programs are defined in terms of desired inputs (budgets), processes (planned instructional programs), and outputs (performance objectives), and of actual inputs (expenditures), processes (actual instructional programs), and outputs (measured pupil performance). In phase four community goal statements for the school are developed. And, in phase five the school's operating programs are compared to, and reconciled with, the community-goal statements. In phase six the planning cycle begins once again in an attempt to bring the school's operating programs closer to the community's goals.

Such a system has several distinguishing characteristics: it is oriented toward outcome of instruction with heavy emphasis on the use of information feedback for continued planning; it explicitly separates the community's responsibility for establishing goals from professional responsibilities for determining instructional programs, while trying to match the two; it calls for program planning at the instructional level, with the meaningful involvement of those who must carry out the plans.

Planning, programming, and budgeting systems represent much more than a new approach to budgeting. Although they call for budgeting and accounting procedures that display financial data according to both object category and program, those who adopt only program budgeting fail to capitalize on the advantages inherent in the technology. The ultimate use of PPBS in schools is to relate expenditures to educational outcomes, and to use the resulting information to improve instructional programs.

Community Assessment

Exhortations to assess the community and to relate educational programs to community needs are certainly not new. To assess and understand a community, however, requires the technical skills of accumulating and displaying data from which valid generalizations about that community can be drawn.

Demographic data, including information on such variables as income level, ethnic background, and occupational status are available from census reports. Although such information does not provide precise information on the attitudes held by community members nor reveal the citizens' goals and aspirations for the education of their children, it does help to identify community groups and their location, a factor in knowing one's community.

More definitive information on the attitudes held by members of various interest groups can be obtained through the use of sampling techniques. Techniques such as public opinion polls have long been used by business firms and candidates for political office. They have seldom been employed by schools, yet they provide an efficient and relatively inexpensive means of maintaining an awareness of the political forces that impinge on the school.

Although it is important to be aware of the forces that currently exist, it is equally important, as Gaynor noted, for the principal to develop a vision of the future. Without a sense of the direction in which social forces are moving, the school would constantly respond in a reactive mode to events generated by the actions of others.

Several techniques for both predicting and directing the future have been developed and used in recent years with moderate success. One of the more promising of these techniques, the Delphi, represents a specialized application of sampling procedures. In essence, this technique employs a series of questionnaires to arrive at consensus among experts regarding some future event. By using questionnaires to replace direct discussion, the technique avoids the undue influence of personal persuasion, the unwillingness of individuals to abandon positions they have taken publicly, and the tendency for majority arguments to produce bandwagon effects.[13]

Although the Delphi technique is most commonly used to predict future events, it is also being employed to derive statements of organizational goals. A major advantage of the technique is that it not only provides a means of reaching consensus on goals but it also enables the user to weigh goal statements, thus establishing goal priorities.

Group Process and Communication Skills

As schools move more and more to using groups both to plan and carry out instructional programs, the limitation of traditional approaches to identifying and solving organizational problems becomes increasingly apparent. The weaknesses of these approaches derive from inappropriate procedures for managing problem-solving groups and from inadequate attention to the difficulties encountered when individuals attempt to communicate their ideas to others.

Standard parliamentary procedures provide an adequate mechanism for enabling a legal body or a large group to take action when it consists of reaching a decision by majority vote. Such procedures are inappropriate and inadequate for use with problem-solving groups, however, since these groups work not to settle an issue by majority vote but, instead, to find ways to reduce discrepancies between an existing situation and a desired situation. Thus, the leader of such a group needs skills to help the participants clarify and verify the current state of affairs, to make explicit the desired state of affairs, and to specify courses of action that will enable the group to move from what exists to what is desired.

Considerable effort in recent years has been expended to improve the problem-solving skills of both leaders and group members. The approach known as Laboratory Training for Organizational Development (OD) represents an attempt to "teach, legitimize, and make normative a systematic, adaptive, and flexible problem-solving sequence."[14] This problem-solving sequence consists of clarifying the problem areas or desirable end states, evaluating the forces acting to keep the problems from moving toward solutions (force-field analysis), setting priorities for increasing or decreasing the forces, planning for action, and evaluating the effects of the actions taken. Organizational training in this mode places heavy emphasis on the acquisition of communication skills, including skills in paraphrasing (making sure that you understand the other person's message), behavior description (describing what you see behaviorally, avoiding inference), description of feelings (not inferences or thoughts), and perception checking (describing to another how you think he is feeling so that he can verify or deny your supposition).

Other efforts are being made to develop materials and procedures to improve group process and communication skills.[15] Certainly this is a critical area of performance in the principal's role.

Management and Organizational Skills

If we accept Barnard's thesis that the role of the executive is the specialized work of maintaining the organization in operation, then it follows that a central task of the administrator is to take the lead in establishing and maintaining an effective organization for carrying out the functions for which the institution exists. This involves establishing appropriate structural arrangements for the functions to be performed and providing adequate incentives to elicit the necessary contributions from members of the organization for the accomplishment of the organization's tasks. The establishment of appropriate structural arrangements involves essentially McIntyre's key responsibilities II, III, and IV: the principal allocates staff personnel to accomplish instructional goals; the principal allocates time and space to accomplish instructional goals; and the principal develops and utilizes materials, equipment, and facilities to accomplish instructional goals.

A number of promising techniques and organizational arrange-

ments for deploying resources have been developed recently to improve schools. Modular scheduling, team teaching, open-space
schools, and instructional aids contribute to the development of students, and an effective principal will be aware of these techniques
and arrangements, of their advantages and limitations. He will also
employ the technical skills involved in preparing budgets, accounting
for expenditures, and maintaining inventories on supplies and equipment, important indications of administrative performance.

Another significant category of management skills, however, has
received relatively little attention to date. It was mentioned by Lipham in that part of Chapter Four related to implementing solutions.
As Lipham points out, even the best decision may founder at the
implementation stage. Skill in monitoring (managing) the implementation of a decision is essential for effective performance in the administrative role. A useful set of tools developed and perfected recently can contribute greatly to this aspect of administrative performance: the network-planning tools of program evaluation and review technique (PERT) and critical path method.

Regardless of the technique chosen, the underlying purpose is to
provide a detailed plan to ensure that all of the necessary activities in
a program will be carried out on schedule. The technique can be used
in managing tasks ranging from the routine and simple to the innovative and highly complex. A brief review of PERT can illustrate the
application of these techniques.[16]

The first step in applying PERT is to subdivide a project or task
into its major work elements. For each work element, a network is
developed consisting of events and activities. An *activity* is a task or
job requiring the utilization of personnel and resources over time,
while an *event* represents the start or completion of an activity.

As the network is developed, relationships among events are
charted so that it is possible to identify dependencies and constraints. Thus, if one event must occur before another activity can
begin, that fact can be noted and diagramed. Estimates are then
made of the time it will take to complete each activity, and from
those estimates it is possible to calculate the total amount of time it
will take to complete the project.

A carefully developed PERT chart provides many advantages in
managing a project. For one thing, it requires the planners to be explicit about what is required to carry out the project, thus minimiz-

ing the chance that important activities will be ignored. It also provides an excellent means for monitoring progress. If it becomes apparent that an event that constrains another activity will be delayed, for example, additional resources can be added to avoid the delay or the project can be rescheduled to accommodate the delay.

Little work has been done to adapt these techniques to the work of the school principal. Thus the presence or absence of such techniques can hardly be used to evaluate a principal's performance. However, training to improve performance should include provisions for developing these and similar management skills.

HUMAN SKILLS

Human skills contribute to an individual's ability to work effectively as a group member. Since the principal holds a unique position in his membership group, the school faculty, the definition of effectiveness as a group member must take into account the specialized roles he is required to perform by virtue of holding that position. Thus, to the extent that the principal is called on to take the lead in building cooperative effort within the faculty, to serve as a mediator between the faculty and the central office, or to set the tone for openness and trust in both formal and informal interpersonal relationships, these factors should be considered in assessing his performance.

Human skills are the most difficult of the three types to deal with in the context of performance. This is partly true because they pervade all aspects of performance. An individual may be unusually competent technically, with highly developed abilities to employ effective processes and procedures. If he cannot relate well to others in a group setting, however, technical competence is of little value. Moreover, human skills are heavily influenced by the individual's personality, by his sense of adequacy or inadequacy, his own fears and aspirations, and his own openness to experience. As Hughes has pointed out, an individual may acquire and employ several human relations techniques, but unless these techniques become a part of him, unless he behaves authentically as he relates to others, he is distrusted and his effectiveness is seriously impaired. Since authenticity is difficult both to assess and to develop, human skills are difficult to identify and improve; they are, nevertheless, crucially important for effective performance. Attempts to assess and improve them must be made.

Since human skills involve an individual's interactions with others, then others' perceptions of the individual's behavior may, perhaps, represent the most appropriate means of assessment. If a principal is viewed by most of the teachers in the school as being considerate, empathetic, and understanding, it can be assumed that his behavior is appropriate in respect to those factors. Of the instruments currently available to obtain this type of information, Halpin and Croft's Organizational Climate Description Questionnaire is most promising.[17]

Another approach to assessing the principal's impact on the tone or climate of the organization also deserves serious attention. It relates to the general question of morale, with specific emphasis on employee satisfaction. Numerous studies made in both industrial and educational settings show a distinction between the factors that contribute to employee satisfaction and those that contribute to employee dissatisfaction.[18] The factors that have consistently been shown to contribute to satisfaction are: a sense of achievement; recognition of others; opportunities to accept responsibility, both for one's own efforts and for the work of others; opportunities for advancement and professional growth. The factors that have just as consistently been shown to contribute to dissatisfaction are: unfair policies and administrative practices; incompetent supervisors; lack of recognition of others; and poor interpersonal relationships with supervisors and administrators.

Two implications of these studies are worth noting. First, the factors that contribute to dissatisfaction tend to center around the administrator and the forces that he controls. Second, unless the conditions that create dissatisfaction are corrected, the factors that create satisfaction tend to be submerged. Thus, the administrator has the potential for both contributing to the dissatisfaction of employees and blocking the emergence of those factors from which employees obtain a sense of satisfaction and fulfillment in their work. The means of obtaining a reasonable measure of employee satisfaction-dissatisfaction are relatively simple and inexpensive to administer, and it would be productive to pursue this approach in assessing the performance of school principals in the realm of interpersonal relationships.

NOTES

1. Andrew W. Halpin, *Theory and Research in Administration* (New York: Macmillan Co., 1966), pp. 81, 86.

2. Chester I. Barnard, *The Functions of the Executive* (Cambridge, Mass.: Harvard University Press, 1958), p. 215.

3. Matthew B. Miles, "Planned Change and Organizational Health: Figure and Ground," in *Change Processes in the Public Schools* (Eugene, Ore.: Center for the Advanced Study of Educational Administration, University of Oregon, 1965), p. 12.

4. Andrew W. Halpin and Don B. Croft, *The Organizational Climate of Schools* (Chicago: Midwest Administration Center, University of Chicago, 1963).

5. Robert L. Katz, "Skills of an Effective Administrator," *Harvard Business Review*, 33 (February 1955), 33-42.

6. *Ibid.*, p. 33.

7. *Ibid.*

8. James G. March and Herbert A. Simon, *Organizations* (New York: John Wiley and Sons, 1959), p. 141.

9. Dan C. Lortie, "Change and Exchange: Reducing Resistance to Innovation," *Administrators Notebook* (Chicago: Midwest Administration Center, University of Chicago), 12 (No. 6, February 1964).

10. March and Simon, *Organizations*.

11. Willis W. Harman, "Nature of Our Changing Society: Implications for Schools," in Philip K. Piele, Terry L. Eidell, and Stuart C. Smith (eds.), *Social and Technological Changes: Implications for Education* (Eugene, Ore.: Center for the Advanced Study of Educational Administration, University of Oregon, 1970).

12. School Planning, Evaluation, and Communications System (SPECS), developed by Terry L. Eidell and John M. Nagle at the Center for the Advanced Study of Educational Administration, University of Oregon.

13. For a more detailed discussion of the Delphi, see Stuart A. Sandrow, *Educational Policy Formulation: Planning with the Focus Delphi and the Cross-Purpose Matrix* (Syracuse, N. Y.: Educational Policy Research Center, Report RR-9, 1972).

14. Daniel Langmeyer, Richard A. Schmuck, and Philip J. Runkel, *Technology for Organizational Training in Schools* (Eugene, Ore.: Center for the Advanced Study of Educational Administration, University of Oregon, August 1971), p. 2.

15. See, for example, the CASEA Progress Report—Ernstspiel, by Francis C. Thiemann and Chester S. Bumbarger.

16. For a thorough discussion of PERT, see Desmond L. Cook, *Program Evaluation and Review Technique: Applications in Education*, Cooperative Research Monograph No. 17 (Washington, D. C.: U.S. Department of Health, Education, and Welfare, Office of Education, 1966).

17. See Chapter Five.
18. See Frederick Herzberg, Bernard Mausner, and Barbara Snyderman, *The Motivation to Work* (New York: John Wiley & Sons, 1959).